EDWARD DORN

EDWARD DORN
TWO INTERVIEWS

Editors: Gavin Selerie and Justin Katko

Published in the United Kingdom in 2012 by
Shearsman Books
50 Westons Hill Drive
Emersons Green
BRISTOL
BS16 7DF

Shearsman Books Ltd Registered Office
30–31 St. James Place, Mangotsfield, Bristol BS16 9JB
(this address not for correspondence)

www.shearsman.com

ISBN 978-1-84861-278-5

Texts and statements by Edward Dorn and Jennifer Dunbar Dorn
copyright © Jennifer Dunbar Dorn, 2012

Preface copyright © Justin Katko, 2012

Texts and statements by J.H. Prynne copyright © J.H. Prynne, 2012

'*The Peak* Interview' copyright © Tom McGauley, Brian Fawcett,
John Scoggan, Stan Persky, and Ralph Maud, 2012

'The Riverside Interview' and 'Circumstance and Shadow-Track'
copyright © Gavin Selerie, 2012

Cover photographs: *(Left)* Edward Dorn at the National Poetry Festival,
Thomas Jefferson College, Allendale, Michigan, June 1973; photograph by
Craig Vander Lende; courtesy of Robert Vas Dias. *(Right)* Edward Dorn at
the Poetry Society / National Poetry Centre, Earl's Court, London, June
1981; photograph by Alan Burgis; courtesy of Gavin Selerie.

Back cover text: from 'The Riverside Interview' (1981).

TABLE OF CONTENTS

7: Preface
    Justin Katko

15: *The Peak* Interview (1971)
    Edward Dorn, Tom McGauley,
    Brian Fawcett and John Scoggan,
    with J.H. Prynne, Stan Persky and Ralph Maud

31: From *The Day & Night Report* (1971)
    Edward Dorn

39: Circumstance and Shadow-Track:
    Introduction to 'The Riverside Interview'
    Gavin Selerie

63: The Riverside Interview (1981)
    Edward Dorn and Gavin Selerie

85: From *Juneau in June* (1980–81)
    Edward Dorn

95: Three Poems and a Draft (1981)
    Edward Dorn

100: Bibliography of Edward Dorn Interviews

101: Biographical Notes

PREFACE

As its title announces, this book collects two interviews with the American poet Edward Dorn. 'The Peak Interview' (1971), conducted by Robin Blaser's students Tom McGauley, Brian Fawcett, and John Scoggan, was published in Simon Fraser University's student newspaper *The Peak*, and contains contributions from J.H. Prynne, Stan Persky, and Ralph Maud. We have followed up the interview with a short selection of texts from *The Day & Night Report* (Dorn's unpublished daybook from 1971), hopefully in advance of a full publication of that work in the near future. 'The Riverside Interview' (1981) was intended for publication in the *Riverside Interviews* series and is supplemented here with an introduction by Gavin Selerie, the interviewer. Following it is a selection of two chapters from Dorn's unpublished prose work *Juneau in June* (1980–81), as well three uncollected poems (including a draft of one of them) from the English magazine *Spectacular Diseases* (1981). The interviews add to what has been available for some time, mostly in Dorn's *Interviews* (1980), and more recently in Joseph Richey's compilation *Ed Dorn Live* (2007); but they also participate in a wider renewal of interest in the work of this singular poet.

2004 saw the publication of a special Dorn issue of the *Chicago Review*, edited by Eirik Steinhoff; as well as the American poetry issue of *Edinburgh Review*, featuring Sam Ladkin's excellent essay on *Gunslinger*. These works benefitted from an early look into Dorn's papers, held in the Thomas J. Dodd Research Center at the University of Connecticut, an archive not catalogued until 2005. A few more scholars have since made forays into those papers, the fruits of which labour are beginning to emerge, amidst the more general enterprise of Dorn publishing. In 2010, Optic Nerve and Birkbeck College released a CD of otherwise unavailable readings, entitled *Idaho Out: Poems 1964–1967*. A special Dorn issue of *Hot Gun!* was published in 2011, edited with an extended introduction by Joshua Stanley, with essays and transcriptions of unpublished or obscure texts, along with poems by contemporary British and American poets. Reitha Pattison's *Edward Dorn: Geography, Capitalism and Cosmology*, forthcoming from Peter Lang, will be the first Dorn monograph since James K. Elmborg's 1998 study of *Gunslinger*. Kyle Waugh is preparing Dorn's *Collected Prose*, and for CUNY's Lost & Found project he is editing the unpublished screenplay from the '60s/'70s, *Abilene! Abilene!*. Other Lost & Found projects include Claudia Pisano's 2009 selection of Dorn's correspondence with Amiri Baraka (which publication promises a forthcoming full collection of the Dorn/Baraka letters) and Lindsey M. Freer's 2012 edition of Dorn's 1981 *Charles Olson Memorial Lectures* (though the second of these three lectures remains available only on *Pennsound*). Matt Hofer, through the University of New Mexico, is preparing a new edition of *The Shoshoneans*. Etruscan Books has this year published an edition of the unfinished long poem *Westward Haut*. And finally, Carcanet Press has just published Edward Dorn's first *Collected Poems* since 1983, edited by Jennifer Dunbar Dorn and co-edited by Reitha Pattison, Kyle Waugh, and myself. A volume of poems not included in the Carcanet publication is being planned by the editors.

That the posthumous *Collected Poems* of a major American poet should be first published in England is testament to the transatlantic asymmetry of concern for Dorn's writing. In part, his international appeal is amplified because, to some extent, he crossed over: in both of the interviews published here, Dorn explicitly reaffirms the importance of his time in England, where all in all he lived on and off for half a decade, in Colchester, London, and Cambridge. Much of his most brilliant work was written or first published in England in the sixties, and as he wrote towards the end of his life, in his introduction to *High West Rendezvous* (1996): "my sojourn in England nearly half a life-time ago... set me on a new course". The shape and speed of Dorn's imagination changed in proportion with the shift of his geographical coordinates. This shift is mapped out in *The North Atlantic Turbine*, Dorn's painful account of cultural disorientation and loss, perhaps the most equally difficult and beautiful of his books. Stating at the opening of '*The Peak* Interview' that *The North Atlantic Turbine* was "one of the most important books, most necessary books I'll ever do", Dorn goes on to say that "I never read it, and I never read from it. Or want to see it." Dorn's contemporaneous recordings of this work are extraordinary,[1] which is not surprising because *The North Atlantic Turbine* is a desperate book, a record of the shock of Dorn's American dealignment (as well as the origin of his most acclaimed work, *Gunslinger*). His refusal to countenance the reckless precision of *The North Atlantic Turbine* four years after its publication has its counterpart monstrosity in America's failure to celebrate one of the greatest products of its strange interior.

The interviews and writing published here span a decade of adjustment for Dorn. The opening strokes of *Gunslinger*, written before 1968, were impatient for their impossible closure in the 1970s. The epigrammatic style characterising *Abhorrences* and earlier books was just beginning to emerge in Dorn's readings and magazine publications; this was a product both of the overflow into Dorn's general poetic consciousness of *Gunslinger's* rolling dialogic comedy, and of his practice of keeping a daybook in 1971. By 1971, Dorn's language was no longer American English, nor was it quite the English with which he began *Gunslinger*. Dorn's first family was effectively left behind, and his teacher Charles Olson lived only ten days into the seventies. Dorn emerged out of the sixties with a new family, formed with his English wife Jennifer Dunbar Dorn (who kept a parallel 1971 daybook, one of the couple's various collaborations). In so many other ways was the continent on which Dorn became a poet in the fifties not the continent he returned to in the late sixties. And accordingly, he did not hesitate to give the full expanse of his "home" a thorough inspection, reading his poetry at venues across the country, teaching and writing in New England, Kansas, Chicago, Ohio, and California (where he spent considerable time with Tom Raworth and the printers who would set the complete *Slinger*), living in cities and towns and mountain retreats across the United States, consuming a wide variety of drugs, travelling through Mexico with his family (who later took a cross-country road trip with J.H. Prynne), returning to England for another teaching stint at Essex, then back to California, and finally landing a permanent job in Colorado.

---

[1] There are two sources for these: the 1967 Livingdisc/Stream Records LP *Edward Dorn reads from The North Atlantic Turbine*, available online at *Ubuweb*; and the Optic Nerve CD *Idaho Out*.

It was in the summer of 1971 that Prynne and the Dorns drove across America, from Boston, through Chicago (where the Dorns were then living) and up across the border to Vancouver. Jennifer Dunbar Dorn's daybook (in Box 39 of Connecticut's Dorn Papers) is, apart from being a literary work in its own right, a useful source of information about that trip. The band of travelers arrived in Vancouver on 20 July, staying for a fortnight as the guests of Stan Persky (who in 1964 was editor of the San Francisco magazine *Open Space*). Persky lived at the York Street Commune, a writers' house in Vancouver's Kitsilano district, which area is named in the first line of Dorn's 24 July poem 'Day Report, 205th day' (p. 32). On top of the writing they all did—parts of Prynne's *Into the Day* were grown if not germinated in Vancouver—their two weeks at York Street were, in certain ways, a busy time. On 27 July, Prynne lectured 'On Maximus IV, V & VI', organised by Ralph Maud; that this now rather infamous talk was improvised gives one a sense of the kind of conversation that must have gone on during Prynne and the Dorns' leisurely drive across the States. On the same day, Stan Persky and the augmented York Street family released the eighth number of *Writing*, a "mass poetry newsprint supplement" inserted into the underground newspaper *Georgia Straight*. Next to a photograph of the Dorn family and Prynne piled up in a "totem pole" in the York Street backyard, the cover of *Writing* 8 is written so as to read *Writing* ∞, reflecting Prynne and Dorn's then interest in the mathematician Georg Cantor. *Writing* ∞ includes work by Robert Duncan, Robin Blaser, and George Stanley, and also includes the Dorns' collaboration 'Door County—South Dakota Time', extracts from Edward Dorn's *Day & Night Report*, his poem 'Thesis', his story 'Of Eastern Newfoundland, Its Inns and Outs', and two poems from Prynne's *Brass*, 'The Blade Given Back' and 'Of Sanguine Fire'.[2] According to references in Jennifer Dunbar

---

[2] Regarding the collages of William Blake's designs and photographs of scientific/natural objects running along the right-hand margins of 'Of Sanguine Fire', which are finely coordinated with the text, note that though the collages throughout *Writing* ∞ have been acknowledged in correspondence with Stan Persky as being made by Persky's partner Brian DeBeck, there is nonetheless a miniscule line of Prynne's handwriting on the first page of 'Of Sanguine Fire'—running beneath 'The Skeleton Re-Animated', one of Blake's illustrations to Robert Blair's poem *The Grave*—which marginalium records the

Dorn's daybook, as well as Dorn and Prynne's correspondence, a critique of *Writing ∞*, potentially written by George Stanley, appeared in the parent organ *Georgia Straight*, even before the invaders from the East could skip town.

Dorn and Prynne each gave readings during their stay in Vancouver, recordings of most of which have recently been unearthed by Fred Wah. On 29 July, at the York Street Commune, Dorn read *Gunslinger: Book I* and selections from *The Day & Night Report*. At Intermedia, on 30 July, Prynne read from *Brass* ('Thinking of You' and 'Royal Fern') and *The White Stones* ('In Cimmerian Darkness', 'Moon Poem', 'The Glacial Question, Unsolved', 'A Dream of Retained Colour', 'Star Damage at Home', 'Frost and Snow, Falling', 'A Stone Called Nothing', and 'Aristeas, in Seven Years'). Following Prynne, Dorn read *Gunslinger: Book II*, opening his reading by way of transition: "We've had the divine, I guess; that's certainly true. Maybe we can have the vulgar now". Again at York Street, on 31 July, Dorn read *The Cycle* and *Gunslinger: Book III (The Winterbook)*, which Dorn had just put the finishing touches on during the course of their road trip, as Dorn and Prynne's correspondence implies). Then on 1 August, at York Street, Prynne read from *Kitchen Poems* ('Numbers in Time of Trouble'), *The White Stones* ('Quality in that Case as Pressure', 'Shadow Songs', 'On the Matter of Thermal Packing', 'Oil', 'From End to End', 'A Sonnet to Famous Hopes', 'The Corn Burned by Syrius', 'Starvation / Dream', 'Crown', and 'As It Were An Attendant'), the entirety of *A Night Square*, and *Brass* ('Es Lebe der König', 'The Kirghiz Disasters', 'The Five Hindrances', and 'Of Sanguine Fire'). The travelers left Vancouver the following day, swinging down to California before returning to Chicago, where Prynne flew out on 23 August, leaving for his friends this handwritten token of a hyper-farewell, an undeniable homage to the author of *The Winterbook*'s 'NIGHTLETTER':

---

city, date, and venue of publication ('Vancouver, Published July 27 by Georgia Straight'). This acknowledgment provides the only textual indication of any of the possibly several (co-)authorships of *Writing ∞*'s visual designs.

> M25423 MSG START/
> unit influx to pre Atlantic
> vector shot dips under 20° to
> exceptionless generalisation, figures
> one and final say again one
> through zero, all channels
> counter/rotate efference Western
> loop refuso. Angle on site
> Response aligned in real time ~~with~~
> azimuth to 5 (set cupric discharge
> on-line at nil sodium level). Print-out
> by terminal fade corrected
> through ~~continental shift~~
> shift to lock on: msg redegraded
> in clear 10 reads 54321 Thanks 00

Now, nearly fifteen years after Edward Dorn's death, with a fuller range of his work and influence pulling slowly into more and more finite view, it is timely to contribute to the body of those texts where he speaks most casually and freely. But Dorn is almost always flirting on the rim of casually dislocating his readers from their precious expectations, as in the jacket note to *The North Atlantic Turbine* (reprinted in the *Collected Poems*), or his introductory note to *The Book of Daniel Drew* (reprinted in *Hot Gun!*), to cite two examples from the late 1960s. But even in those cases, there is still the Dornian sense of formality and occasion, the voice of this man addressing himself to this world. That sense is not so present in his interviews and lectures, when he is addressing himself to the people before him. There is less of the universal; and for this, Dorn's interviews will not always be the most reliable tool for the task of sorting out which of his writing to study for instruction and which of it to understand as a mockery of its author's visionary intellect and passion for truth. Amiri

Baraka has likened Edward Dorn's mind to a buzz saw; its hum is a sound the world could do with a Hell of a lot more of.

*

The editors wish to thank: Jennifer Dunbar Dorn, for making available the *Juneau in June* extracts and for granting us permission to publish the work presented here; J.H. Prynne, for providing files from his Dorn correspondence, from which 'The Peak Interview', and two poems from *The Day & Night Report* were transcribed, and Prynne's own 'NY251423MSGSTART/' sourced; Robert Vas Dias, for providing Dorn correspondence files related to *Manchester Square*; Melissa Watterworth Batt, at the University of Connecticut's Thomas J. Dodd Research Center, for locating and making available the draft of 'How Small Can Awesome Get?'; Neil Pattison, for serendipitously producing the sixth issue of *Spectacular Diseases*; Stan Persky, for information on the *Georgia Straight Writing Supplement* and the Dorns' and Prynne's visit to Vancouver; Brian Fawcett, for his recollections of the same; Fred Wah, for information about Dorn and Prynne's Vancouver readings; Tony Power at Simon Fraser University's Bennett Library, Matt ffytche, Pete Smith, and Ian Brinton, for helping to source copies of the *Georgia Straight Writing Supplement*; Richard Berengarten, Kyle Waugh, Michael Tencer, Colin Still, and Ralph Maud, for various information or help with the provisional bibliography at the end of this book; and Keston Sutherland, Christina Chalmers, Keith Tuma, Ian Patterson, and Isolde Mayer for their helpful comments on drafts of this preface.

THE PEAK INTERVIEW

Edward Dorn interviewed by
Tom McGauley, Brian Fawcett and John Scoggan,
with J.H. Prynne, Stan Persky and Ralph Maud

Vancouver, 22 July 1971

'Edward Dorn', *The Peak*, 18.4 (Burnaby Mountain, Simon Fraser University, British Columbia, 4 August 1971), 8-9. Square brackets are present in the original publication.

Opposite: Pictured at the York Street Commune, Vancouver, July 1971, are (left to right): trade union activist and York Streeter Cliff Andstein, Jennifer Dunbar Dorn, Maya Dorn, Edward Dorn, and Kidd Dorn; courtesy of Jennifer Dunbar Dorn.

Ed Dorn is, as Stan Persky put it, the last of the big daddy writers to come to Vancouver. Tom McGauley, Brian Fawcett and John Scoggan did the interview on Thursday afternoon, July 22, 1971, on the front balcony of the York Street commune, where the sounds of the traffic and of George Bowering's Miltonic bellowing from down the street drowned out a good part of the conversation. Jeremy Prynne was there, as were Stan Persky and Ralph Maud. The interview was, as consequence, hard to transcribe and a certain lack of continuity will be apparent. We had the choice of trying to interview Dorn again, in a quieter but doubtless less easy context, but decided that the most interesting questions we asked were so uncouth they would have been impossible to ask a second time. All reference to George Bowering or other gases have been expunged from the text.

* * *

McGauley: One of the lines of one of the poems I read in *The North Atlantic Turbine* says, "the lonely man with a masonic ring" etc. What part does that kind of particularity play, the masonic sense in Idaho, etc.?

Dorn: Yeah. Well, if there were a bestiary of, and there should be, books of poems in the last fifty years or so, *The North Atlantic Turbine* would be in it, as one of the beasts. Because it's like, made of the parts of a verse practice which was ending, in that way, so strong, that it couldn't stop before that book got written. I just look at the book as a curiosity. There are parts of it, like the preoccupation with somebody like a Mason, which would be an American thing to do, actually. All that kind of memory force got in, warped into a context in which I thought at the time I was able to speak to the English people... a great mistake, actually, to speak to a foreign people. Not really, I mean, that works both ways—you speak to the language you're writing, that's all... So those habits would just come forward from Idaho. Cause that was the place I'd been before. I mean that book was that... well, there's other things, that shot at J. Paul Getty, things like that. All of it strange. Maybe one of the most important books, most necessary books I'll ever do. But I never read it, and I never read from it. Or want to see it.

SCOGGAN: Why?

DORN: Well, if you write like I do, which is on the basis of this certain quota of mistakes made public, made overtly public, it's just there, and I don't mind, but I don't want to sign it, actually, when somebody comes up and says, wow, here's a book of yours—I don't want to see it.

PRYNNE: But you wouldn't mind writing your address on the front of the cover?

DORN: Not at all, that would be perfectly okay. I think anybody can write my address on the cover of *The North Atlantic Turbine*. I wouldn't flinch.

FAWCETT: Why did you go to England?

DORN: To visit Jeremy Prynne. It's like, I'm working in the teaching trade, so that was a job that turned out to be 5 years.

FAWCETT: You're back in North America now?

DORN:: Yah.

FAWCETT: Do you include New York and Seattle as parts of the same country? I'm trying to speak out of my sense of our country which is totally regional. I see someone from Toronto as like from Upper Canada, and they are more foreign than someone from Seattle.

DORN: You know, I have an attitude which is extremely difficult for the Canadians I've talked to to dig. My sense of home is hemispheric, not national. So I really don't feel like I'm not at home in Canada, nor Mexico, nor New York, although the terms which are enforced by not being there, are much more radical obviously.

FAWCETT: What about England?

DORN: I did not feel like it was a foreign country while I was there. When I was in England I felt that America was a foreign country.

SCOGGAN: I'd like to know what does make these kinds of ties.

DORN: Well, look, it isn't very difficult. It's how you feel the landscape... somewhere north of Lake Superior the rivers start flowing into the Arctic Ocean. And somewhere south... I mean I feel that the air comes down from Wisconsin, and it's cold. And when it comes up from Gary, it's not so good. Those are much more practical day-to-day ways you feel where you are, than a boundary that runs from International Falls, which doesn't mean anything to me at all. Now, I'm told that only an American can afford to express this attitude, because it derives from a kind of arrogance of hemispheric conception.

SCOGGAN: How can you talk about such a vast conception?

DORN: Well, if you have a world image, and you do, in your head, you feel that this is a particular hemisphere, like it's the thinnest, and it's the new one, and it's the isolated one, and it's like quite instant, like our consciousness of it. There is no emotional or intellectual backlog. It's right here, I mean we can say absolutely everything we know in two or three phrases, and you just keep repeating them. I'm talking about what's common to the psychic potential of anybody who registers here. That could be my mother as much as me. Nationalism in this hemisphere distorts what the hemisphere is, by reference to the western world. When that happens all sorts of scapegoats are immediately thrown up, like false images, you know, do not erect false images. It's almost like a religious term. It's a difficult position to argue because it obviously flies in the face of lots of practical and immediate feelings. Paranoia is a real thing. I know that, I just believed those things have to be worked out on a hemispheric scale, as well as the local. You know, the national is the stretch where the line gets weak and the whole thing buckles... which is the nation... you go right from the ultra small to the ultra large. For instance, on that national thing, you get people south of the border. I'd actually like to think I'm from Mexico when I come to Canada... who are going to believe that Nixon is going to Peking as an absolutely initial contact between this hemisphere and Peking. They've never been told and they never will, that Canada has been all along selling China wheat, and there's been real Chinamen in Vancouver, and all sorts of things like that. They don't know it now, and they never will know it. I'm using that as an example of where, when it's put in that national thing, that kind of tragedy happens. And that's really a tragedy of the consciousness, not for you, but for south of the border.

McGAULEY: Where do you see yourself moving now, in relation to your own ground?

DORN: Well you must know I've been writing a continuous poem since about 1967–68 called *Gunslinger*, and I haven't really written anything else. I write *Gunslinger* all the time, maybe to relieve the boredom.

McGAULEY: How would you share that process with someone who finds it difficult to understand what it means to be working on one long poem?

DORN: I share it co-terminously with the writing. The method is to reveal [drowned out] ... in the text itself... the audience [of the poem *Gunslinger I* and *II*] is quite small... I reject mimeographing the poem in this sense because the form just won't take the pseudo-formality of the poem... in order to make that register, that it's a kind of comment on present formalism, it has to be a [...] printing, and registered very well. I think some people would disagree with that, but I feel it anyway, that it mustn't be dashed off.

FAWCETT: Couldn't you put instructions in them, how to steal the book?

DORN: Well, I really don't mind who steals it. If it's there, people obviously have the choice of buying or stealing it. That's actually their problem. But the cost I tried to do something about by changing publishers, from a publisher who is a very good publisher and gave me a kind of printing I liked a lot, but who has an operational commitment that I don't find useful, in terms of this poem, to a publisher who will give a good printing, but who tends to be slow, but with whom I tend to see eye to eye on prices and so forth.

SCOGGAN: Does *Gunslinger* come out of your experiences with the Shoshone Indians?

DORN: No.

SCOGGAN: It comes from that part of the country, doesn't it?

DORN: Yeah. Basically Idaho, Nevada, Utah. No, it came out of, again like, the American far west, which is the land of my imagination, not my home. It's like, you know, my adolescent excursions went through there, when I was fifteen, sixteen, going to L.A., when I was in high school. It was my first experience abroad, which is to say, out of Illinois.

PERSKY: You continue to write short stories, along that...

DORN: Yeah, I mean prose is another thing. Yeah, I'm interested in doing that once in a while. It's like going out and chopping logs or something.

FAWCETT: You see it as that?

DORN: Oh yeah, completely. I'm not a prose writer. I mean there are great prose writers.

PERSKY: Current?

DORN: Yeah, sure. Tom Veitch is a great prose writer. Very current. Did you read the *Tom Veitch Magazine*?... Yeah, you'd say Douglas Woolf, maybe, except that he's been at it for a long time, and he wouldn't come up as a startling new assertion about what's being done.

PERSKY: Right. If I ask anyone I know about the books that do come up, they don't extend very far. Somebody says *The Island* or *The Gold Diggers*, or who's writing or however you want to describe it.

DORN: I think it proves you have to get some sense of value to say something about it. Because it is, you know, it pours out, I mean it's not... for instance Michael McClure writes prose very well, what little I've read of *The Adept*. And I don't know whether you'd say that's great or not. I mean certainly it seems that prose is being written. But again, that's not his primary concern, I don't think. And I don't know the primary concern of Tom Veitch, except that he writes a lot, he's very fluent, you know...

FAWCETT: Okay. Who was the last great prose writer in America?

DORN: The last? Tom Veitch.

FAWCETT: Prior to Tom Veitch.

PRYNNE: Thomas Jefferson.

DORN: Tom Jefferson.

FAWCETT: I don't know whether I'm getting this out of *The Shoshoneans*, or whether this comes out of my own head, but when you and Lucas went down amongst the Shoshones, did you have that book of Agee's in mind?

DORN: Lucas did, I didn't. I wanted to write a book, like. We talked about that too, actually. He thought that I should... Which wasn't an argument really, because he saw very quickly that the nature of the people we were in contact with was so radically difficult and distant. I mean really, when Kerouac and—what's his name, the guy who did the pictures—Frank, that was like another "On the Road" shot, you know with Americans. In fact it was the Americans. Well, the problem with the Indians is that they don't like to be thought of as Americans. They don't like to be thought of as some place along the road, because their attitude is, that they're where they're at. So it's not as if they're characters sitting by an interesting-looking filling station, with precisely weather-beaten faces or that kind of light in the afternoon. The difference is a different proposition altogether. So we didn't do a Robert Frank/Jack Kerouac shot. But then Lucas wasn't Robert Frank and I wasn't Jack Kerouac anyway. So what happened was the book got written and the pictures got taken. Leroy Lucas is a really conscientious worker, as a photographer, and he got right down to dust, works very fast and has a kind of wholesome sense of what to take. When the negatives came up for selection, the editor who contracted for the book had gone to another publisher and there was nobody left who took an interest in the book. So they were just arbitrarily selected by some sub-editor. And the choices were totally bad. I mean I can't think of one that was in the book that couldn't have been better chosen.

FAWCETT: What about the one of the old man on the bed?

DORN: That was just a freaky shot in Elko. That was in Elko.

FAWCETT: But the interesting thing there was the kind of contortions that you went through in order to be able to talk about, and to, the old man.

DORN: Well, see, that... the old man was a Robert Frankism, that preoccupation with the weird and... which I detest, actually.

SCOGGAN: Isn't that what you're talking about in the *Gunslinger*? He goes around and he finds an old man on a bed, and he draws and describes him and that's it? And then you're left with this dead Indian on a bed and that's his place.

FAWCETT: No, no. His whole attack is on description.

SCOGGAN: I know the whole attack is on description, but that book, *The Shoshoneans*, is, because of the editorial policy.

DORN: I'm a great describer because I've got that habit. But I'm not *Gunslinger*. I mean he does it. He does it. That's why I need him because he's really very primitive.

FAWCETT: The only time he does it is with the brilliantine stranger, who asks for it.

DORN: Well, is there any interest around here in Poetry? Do people get together and give readings?

FAWCETT: Well, it comes and goes. There's been a reasonably active thing going on, Stan claims, and I've never taken measure. He says this is a very good city. I don't know. I've never been in any others.

PERSKY: Right. I can live here.

DORN: How many good writers are there in Vancouver?

PERSKY: Six. That's plenty. You find half a dozen people you can talk to, you got plenty.

DORN: In a city this size, that's true. Overpopulated.

PERSKY: Right. And there are more than enough people that are interested; who fall in love all the time.

FAWCETT: I don't know if this is an insult, but…

DORN: I can tell you after you say it…

FAWCETT: Most of the response that I've heard in Vancouver as a writer lately, is through the *Gunslinger* poem. I couldn't get off on it, I got off on *Hands Up!*, but not *The North Atlantic Turbine*, probably because of what you said about it. *Gunslinger*—everybody's fascinated by it, but there's a lot of trouble with it. Like I was introduced to it through the people from Buffalo. But when I first read it I got very angry…

DORN: It was supposed to make that happen.

FAWCETT: I thought it was like… I'm really into it now, really cut my head off… I thought there was a lot of stuff going on that was simply flogging things that were going on—you know, just like so current, and I got angry I guess for that reason, it was too easy.

DORN: Well, that's a kind of perverted idea, that literature could be heard. I don't know. What's wrong with current? I mean I refuse to use a language which is calculated backward in time so as to appear not current. I mean absolutely.

FAWCETT: No, I don't mean it in that sense. Just that it seemed current in the commercial, lousy sense. Things like "Tampico bombers" and stuff like that.

DORN: But that's not current. Nobody says that. I mean, look, you must recognize that this is a… I mean, you can say other things about it. I mean, I'm happy because nobody wants to, necessarily, so I will. That's like, inventive, and that's not current. I mean the practice of invention in literature is not current. So in that sense it's not current. I would take it as an insult that people dug only the prose, because I'm a poet. As a matter of fact it's not fair to even say that to me, because if you write, you write anything, it doesn't actually matter what somebody likes or not.

FAWCETT: Yeah. I didn't mean to lay it down as that kind of remark. It's just that *Rites of Passage*, again, seems so comprehensible. I can plough through the poetry, I go through, but it's tougher.

DORN: Why? It's comprehensible because it's a dumb young

English being practiced by a man that was at that point, wanted so desperately to make a substantial and wide table of statement that there was no other way to do it. So, I mean, that's what the exercise of the mind was at that particular point. Now, unlike *The North Atlantic Turbine*, because that as an act, was very true. But on the other hand that's not the kind of prose for myself. I don't write prose like that now.

MAUD:: Is there any way in which we can take over. From the Lairds. I mean is there, I mean if there isn't an awareness of something?

DORN: No. We've already taken over from Melvin Laird. Melvin Laird is a monster who is not allowed his monstrousness. That's in effect taken over. I mean there's the venom in his fangs, but the holes out of which the venom of his fangs have come, have been plugged. He cannot, in other words, have his whole chew in Southeast Asia. That represents a defeat for his category…

MAUD: How does this come about?

DORN: Well, recently, there are really manifestations of it, like recently it came about because there's a power structure struggle, you know in the New York Times, B.C. Actually the power struggle is inside Harvard—Rostow and Ellsberg. What's this guy's name, Ellsberg?

MAUD: Did Ginsberg have anything to do with it?

DORN: Ginsberg? Oh, well, I don't know. No, I mean, he's at Columbia. I mean he's like Columbia, isn't he? That never was a power seat, Columbia.

MAUD: I mean Ginsberg in the 'Wichita Vortex Sutra' declaring the end of the war.

DORN: Yes, I mean, but that would be like a mistake Columbia would make. You can do it, but nobody necessarily gives a shit. But his is being questioned in a real sense, where the power is really at. And people are being prosecuted for it. This is serious. At least, it's this charade that's quite serious.

PRYNNE: Exactly. I thought you may have had a temporary aberration, Mr. Dorn.

SCOGGAN: And Ginsberg's attempt…

DORN: I don't really think it's got anything to do… Ellsberg is the one.

SCOGGAN: Well, he made up his own action in delivering them forward. It's a kind of invention that he's using in exposing these to the public. And isn't that…

DORN: I don't know, like, the cover story on this, like what his reasons were.

PRYNNE: Well, he didn't make up anything. It comes out of the papers available to the public. He did nothing but slide in that groove. That's an automaton, in spite of all the moral expectations that you might have about that particular kind of intellectually calculated martyrdom. He's obviously got to be a boring man and everything he says from now on right to the day when he either finally goes free or is incinerated, he's got to be as boring as dishwater. It's all been written down in the annals of 19th Century Harvard. There's nothing he could add to it. How could he?

DORN: Yeah, except that he re-enacted the script. I think that's his virtue, that he's playing some kind of a 19th Century man. He's not laying himself open to any kind of attack at all.

PRYNNE: It's a very straight and authentic reproduction.

FAWCETT: Yeah, but like you said, he's not telling anybody anything new. I haven't heard him say one thing that's news.

DORN: That shit's been on the boards since 1958 or something. Did you ever read the *National Guardian* newspaper? They were talking about all that stuff back then.

SCOGGAN: It's all been written out before. This has all been played before. I think this is what... what is the act of poetry trying to do... Is it trying—I mean isn't it valid to draw up the old scripts and work on them again? And present something the way Ginsberg does, or the way you could, or the way any of us could, rather than presenting the power structure as it is, as the reality that exists as it is and getting down to cold hard facts of what we see. Isn't that a possibility, of that kind of invention, idealistic invention, that might live?

DORN: This date.

FAWCETT: It's like that movie *Little Murders* right? Which everybody I know said is very hip politically, and I saw it as a wholly liberal movie. What Feiffer does is set up the situation so he can tell everything like it is, some kind of magical proposition.

DORN: That's like in the cartoons so they won't be able to give him competition. Like, question and answer.

FAWCETT: So somehow if we propose the realistic shittiness of things it'll somehow be made right, God knows through what means, and that's really in that movie.

DORN: Well, of course, that's not going to happen.

SCOGGAN: That's the question, then, where does that rightness come from.

DORN: The only way you can have it is for the mind to be entertained by the body. And that's all, really. There's a quote, like, I exist only for the entertainment of the mind, unquote, my body. I mean that can be anything, really. I mean the content. But I think that whole content question is now absolutely over. It's over. I mean, it's not even a question. There aren't any decisions about content. That's clear. I'm kind of insisting on that, that no more decisions be made about content.

MAUD: What do you mean when you say there's no question about content? It's obvious what the content is? And therefore we don't discuss it, or that we can't discuss it, or it will become everything?

PRYNNE: Oh, I see epigraphs that are just waiting to be...

DORN: It's on that slope over there. [points to North Shore] It comes on at night and you can suddenly see it. It's just it's open, that's all. It's not even a question.

FAWCETT: How can we talk about form if questions of content are no longer relevant?

DORN: Form is an extension of content, or something like that. Well, Olson wasn't even really talking about that at all. That was just like a formula or statement. No, I mean like the larger problem, actually, is what's important to say. Which was a product of... it was that preoccupation with formal means through the mid '50s to recently, and which has so engrossed criticism, what ever that is, couldn't make itself heard, and so you miss the other side of the exchange. But it was always there. And now it's no longer important. I mean because the mind has become active and interesting now. I think thinking was thought to be more interesting earlier. Now, the mind itself is interesting, what it can do, what it can produce, what it's capable of entertaining us with. And I think that's so interesting that I'm not really interested in how people write any more, at all. Not at all. Radically not at all. I'm really interested in what they're giving me, and I don't care how. I don't care how at all.

MAUD: That doesn't mean to say you read everything, though, does it?

DORN: No, you don't care how people write, that's the point. The conclusion to that doesn't mean to say that you will read everything. Something happens when you read some things.

PRYNNE: Well, how doesn't exclude all the other interrogative pronouns—why or what or who or when, etc.

FROM
THE DAY & NIGHT
REPORT (1971)

Edward Dorn

Edward Dorn and Jennifer Dunbar Dorn both kept daybooks in 1971, publishing their 'September Entries' in parallel columns in *Tansy*, 5, ed. John Moritz (Lawrence: Spring/Summer 1972). Edward Dorn published his own entries in several magazines, including *Writing* ∞. Dorn variously refers to this work as *The Day Report*, *The Day & Night Book*, and *The Day & Night Report*. A considerable amount of it remains unpublished: as manuscript in the original daybook and in Dorn's correspondence.

Opposite: Front cover of *Writing: Georgia Straight Writing Supplement*, 8, eds Stan Persky and Dennis Wheeler (Vancouver, 27 July 1971); the constituents of the totem pole may be described in the shorthand of their personal names, from top to bottom: Maya Dorn, Kidd Dorn, Jennifer Dunbar Dorn, Edward Dorn, and J.H. Prynne; image reproduction courtesy of Simon Fraser University, Bennett Library, Special Collections/Rare Books, Contemporary Literature Collection.

Day 77 Thursday 18 March

This morning Night presented her final
idea to me and I opened my eyes. Driving Snowe.
I began to realize a poem from my sleep called

      Parmenides in Magpieform

    He poked his head
and walked around
    while he said there is
      nothing I have said
and Nothing
      I have said is black & white
Why are you in drag
    he read behind my blind
This dress as you can see
    he answered me
was put on
for the party in your mind
and true to my philosophy
I am the last to go
    Good Light

And then he handed me
the menu inside a chinese utility warp

    Boiled Fishing Pole on a bed of Fried Ironing Bloard

16 June

Remember those bad vibes at Goldblatts?
Well, now they're on sale—2 for a quarta

You can get the rest of the year
for a dolla ninety-eight I hear

173rd day—192 follow

A possible apocrypha of Bean (Been
 (which reached me via Alien Signal Band 23)

    "His wrists were bound
    behind his back[1.]
    with diphthongs
    soaked in military secrets
    and held together[2.]
    by an array of green chicklets

1. This is technically impossible—a Bean has no front or back

2. I.e., of course, the Bean circuitry is "locked" along an array of green chicklets

---

Editors' note: 'Day 77 Thursday 18 March' is part of the sequence containing Days 1–79, under the heading 'from The Day Report', in *Caterpillar*, 15/16, ed. Clayton Eshleman (April–July 1971), 182–200. '16 June' and '173rd day—192 follow' are part of the sequence containing Days 92–181, under the heading 'from The Day & Night Book', in *All Stars*, ed. Tom Clark (Santa Fe and New York: Goliard and Grossman, 1972), 101–31.

Easter Sunday

Parade: two protomen inside brown suits
throw their cases of poisoned
bubblegum in the back seat of their yaller
car with the footlong wire in the exact
center of the trunklid. They fasten their belts
and lock into the traffic

April 13 Jefferson 1743

104th, 14 April

President assassinated 1865

O'Hare afternoon acid lounge

Creeley from North Carolina
unnerneath a knitted temple cap
moved in a white light trip
to the nearest bar

Editors' note: The poems from 'Easter Sunday' (Day 101) to 'Eighteen April, Low Sunday' (Day 108) are a continuous part of the sequence in *All Stars* (1972). In 'Eighteen April, Low Sunday', Dorn has "STARING" with one 'R' in both *All Stars* and the archival typescript (Box 38, Folder 623, Edward Dorn Papers, Archives & Special Collections at the Thomas J. Dodd Research Center, University of Connecticut Libraries). Though we have not removed the original asterisks around "COCAINE GREEN", we have nonetheless interpreted them to signify bold type.

Eighteen April, Low Sunday

(a small entertainment for Paul Dorn
on his birthday

You can tell where you were
by going outside.
    When you return
    You can tell where you were
from going back in

        Woodstock 60098

So take a seat. You better check this one out.

    NOW PLAYING AT THE PANTHEON THEATRE

      * COCAINE GREEN *

    STARING—G. Washington, as the Symbol
        i.e., Worthless
    with—T. Jefferson, as the company queer
      –A. Lincoln, as the man from Nowhere
      who takes the blame for Everything
      –A. Hamilton, as the bag man
      –A. Jackson, as his bigger brother
      –U.S. Grant, as "Where it's at"
      –And Introducing

        Dr. Benjamin Franklin Zeus
        as the   hip   recluse

Day Report, 205th day

At Kitselano Beach there is a tidal Tank
Where the women swim with caps on
They are pre-emminently Noradian
in their one piece costumes only

For their excellent health is built
like the many windowed creatures
who loaf around the bay a
protein chain gang drawn from one Bank

and the kid makes his felicitous trips
over the grass and along the ledge
Where the People notice his delicate balance
While they check out the fact of his little Crank

From *The Day & Night Report* (1971)

On first reading *The Glacial Question, Unsolved,* again

For J.H.P. Vancouver 27 July

There are a legion of poets
and like
with any legion the work
is fixed and secondary
a ride in the desert
spent days, one at a time
the serial is in some ways
perfect for a legion

and of the poets prancing
in the academy stock
talking into the face of the clock
only Prynne has the wit to compose
The Pleistocene Rock!

Editors' note: 'Day Report, 205th Day' and 'On first reading *The Glacial Question, Unsolved,* again' (Day 208) are transcribed from a letter from Dorn to J.H. Prynne (13 September 1971) [2 pp., MS], in the possession of J.H. Prynne.

Day 266

At 8:45 AM I rode with Donald Hall and a friend of his to the Pioneer high school in Ann Arbor. The school laid a yellow brick 1949 vision in my mind. Immediately inside the doors I saw the trophy case full of engraved cups and spreading from both sides of my head in a perspective to infinity the Vertical lines of the lockers. The arrogant presumption of the smell of 1949 came into my nostrils. My knees shook and my forehead throbbed and a sharp weakening of the muscle fibre spread throughout my body. This vast extortion lasted 10 seconds and left behind it a frothing mouth European guard dog patrolling ceaselessly the fences of my stomach. Was that the Principle? The effect leaned casually back and put its feet on my face which it assumed was a footstool. Make yourself at home. Apparently, nothing has changed. The boys and girls of the 10th and 11th grades. The girls smile. They smile at me and the guard dog yelps. I can't even wave goodbye to it. The lady with the permanent who is their teacher, and who was my teacher many times, asks them, prompts them, to respond more. One girl breathes "shit" so you can hear it, the girls around her giggle and pop their Bubble gum. I wish I had some.

Editors' note: 'Day 266' is transcribed from Dorn's daybook: Box 40, Thor Notebook, Edward Dorn Papers, Archives & Special Collections at the Thomas J. Dodd Research Center, University of Connecticut Libraries. Note that the reading described here seems to have taken place on Day 264 (21 September 1971), though it is described on the page for Day 266.

CIRCUMSTANCE AND SHADOW-TRACK: INTRODUCTION TO 'THE RIVERSIDE INTERVIEW'

Gavin Selerie

This dialogue was part of the *Riverside Interview* series of extended conversations with poets. It was recorded after dinner in central London, where Dorn's parents-in-law resided, on 16 July, 1981. Their spacious flat on the fourth floor of Bentinck Mansions was one block away from Manchester Square and the Wallace Collection. There was much lively discussion around the dinner table before our interview in an adjacent room, which ended with the resolution to pursue matters further at a subsequent meeting. I remember walking back late to the tube with Nicholas, son of John Dunbar and Marianne Faithfull.

As Jennifer Dunbar Dorn recalls:

> It was the summer of the Royal Wedding and the Brixton Riots, and I remember people asking, "So you're here for the wedding?" We were in Cambridge, staying at J.H. Prynne's Ferry Path house for a few days, maybe a week. Apparently we attended the Raworths' son Ben's trial—with 3 other young men—accused of causing a pub fight, I think. Their daughter Lisa was in the Brixton riots and we published her letter in *Rolling Stock* #1.
>
> We stayed in a house overlooking the Amstel in Amsterdam for 3 weeks—our children were 10 and 12—and then spent much of the summer in Bentinck Street.[1]

This was a period in which Ed Dorn's writing was particularly attuned to harsh political circumstances: the overlapping programmes of Reagan and Thatcher served as a catalyst for his mix of on-the-hoof reportage and honed aphorism.

---

[1] Email to the author, 5 November, 2010. See also Dunbar Dorn's piece about the summer of 1981, 'Comin' Like a Ghosttown', published in *Zephyr*, 2 (Spring 1982). Dorn appeared, with Edward Kamau Brathwaite and Chinua Achebe, at the Cambridge Poetry Festival on 7 June, 1981, when the texts were drawn exclusively from *Yellow Lola*.

Dorn had not read here since the year 1974–75, spent mainly in London and Cambridge.[2] Now, a little way into the next decade, he gave two readings in London, at the Institute of United States Studies on 16 June, and at the Poetry Society, Earl's Court, on 19 June. At the former he read two chapters of a prose work, *Juneau in June* (which stemmed from the previous summer spent in Alaska), *Captain Jack's Chaps* (in a slightly fuller version than that later published) and poems from *Yellow Lola*. At the latter he read parts of *Recollections of Gran Apachería*, *Hello, La Jolla*, *Yellow Lola* and *Captain Jack's Chaps*. Both events also featured the squib about Caspar Weinberger's visit to Europe, 'How Small Can Awesome Get?' The voicing of these texts provided some background for the interview.

I had envisaged the interview moving from its focus on earlier work and influences to discussion of more recent procedures. The track would not be simply chronological but, rather, looping in its course, enabling continuities and contrasts to become apparent. When we met again later in July I provided a list of further questions and areas for discussion but somehow we didn't get anything else down on tape. There was much else to explore, particularly

---

[2] Eric Mottram's account of Dorn's reading at the National Poetry Centre on 17 February, 1974 gives a vivid impression of this previous phase: "A poet's voice performs a composition out of his body, and is a visual as well as an acoustic act.... [Dorn] came in dressed in a light grey pin-cord suit of a 1950's cut, wearing sharply pointed brown shoes, his not very long hair in a short bunch at the neck, and holding his books in a white and blue bandana. He opened the knot, spread the square on the table, took up his books, and used the bandana to mop his brow—which he did throughout the reading. He read clearly and emphatically from the complete *Gunslinger* series, then from his manuscript tome—faltering, losing his place, peering at his handwriting in a new work apparently spread throughout the ledger, and finally read the whole of *Recollections of Gran Apachería*: it was a magnificent performance. Dorn stood well into the audience space, looking directly at the people, and at the conclusion paused for a good half minute while we regarded each other in silence before he signalled the end of the reading. This, too, was part of the action..." ('"Declaring a Behaviour": The Poetry Performance', in *Rawz*, 1, nd [1977]).

Dorn's reciprocal relationship as writer with J.H. Prynne, the shift away from a single lyric voice in *Gunslinger* and the influence of eighteenth century satire upon more recent poems. Another topic was the love lyric, a form handled differently, it seemed, by Dorn and Creeley. When I sent a transcript to Ed he said he wanted to re-draft some or most of his responses and we developed a plan to do this by post over an extended period. Earlier he had agreed that we could draw on his responses to questions and introductions to poems from the Poetry Society reading, which I had taped. This somewhat anticipated the approach which I adopted for the Tom McGrath volume (1983) where I layered interview texts with phone conversation notes, jottings in pubs and cafes, letters from Tom and further responses to questions.[3] The aim was to preserve the live ambiance while achieving solidity of detail and a certain elegance of expression. It was the opposite of what, say, William V. Spanos did in 'Talking with Robert Creeley'.[4]

I sent Dorn a series of supplementary questions, leading out of the discussion of the harmful effects of Romanticism at the end of the taped interview. These embraced such issues as performance, street language and mass culture, publishing contexts, translation and travel writing. There were specific inquiries about Dorn's interaction with Prynne, Tom Raworth, Gordon Brotherston and Stuart Montgomery. In addition, George Butterick supplied a detailed Dorn bibliography to be included at the end of the volume. This was an ambitious project and Ed delayed responding, while I grew increasingly busy with other projects. There was a hiatus in our correspondence. By the end of 1985 I had run out of space, energy and funds for any continuing publication of the Riverside series. This left extended conversations with Robert Creeley, Cid Corman and Theodore Enslin in the can, plus shorter talks with Amiri Baraka and Dorn. (I had tried to persuade Tom Raworth

---

[3] Gavin Selerie, ed., *The Riverside Interviews 6: Tom McGrath* (Binnacle Press, 1983). McGrath discusses Dorn and his work, pp. 90-1, recalling that he did a long review of *Geography* for *Peace News* (25 September, 1966).
[4] *Boundary 2*, VI: 3; VII: 1 (Spring/Fall 1978).

to participate but, as I recall, he felt that he had said enough about relevant topics in his interview with Barry Alpert, published in *Vort*.)

Over the intervening years I maintained occasional contact with Dorn, mainly via readings which he gave in London at the Diorama and other venues.[5] The interview was not quite forgotten but we had both moved on. I included a brief extract in the revised, expanded version of my Olson monograph in *American Poetry: The Modernist Ideal*.[6] Then, some years after Dorn's death, I consulted J.H. Prynne about the viability of publishing the extant text. He felt that, if Jennifer Dunbar Dorn was agreeable, it might be a worthwhile venture; she offered the necessary encouragement. I owe the final impetus for publication to William Rowe, who put me in touch with Justin Katko.

The interview published here is taken from the original transcript, which I have checked against the surviving tape and found to be accurate. It includes some hesitancies and disjunctures which, I suspect, Dorn would have bridged or re-angled. I regret not pushing further to bring this project to fruition during the poet's lifetime.

A useful navigation light is Dorn's suggestion that I should draw attention to the interview he did with Tom Clark, published in *Little Caesar*, 11 (1981). In some respects this forms a counterpart to the dialogue with Clark published as the opening section of *Views* (1980). According to the summary of The Thomas Clark

---

[5] These include: the East West Gallery, W11, reading on 5 June, 1995, which unveiled parts of *Langue D'oc Around the Cloc*, as *Languedoc Variorum* was then titled; the launch of *High West Rendezvous* (Etruscan Books/West House Books) at the Troubadour, Earl's Court, on 28 October, 1996, featuring sections of *Languedoc Variorum*; and the moving performance at the Diorama, 21 December, 1998, when, by request, *Recollections of Gran Apachería* was revisited. I could not attend the event at Compendium Books, 4 June, 1993, presumably a launch for *Way West*.
[6] ed. Clive Bloom and Brian Docherty (Macmillan, 1995).

Papers at Washington University, St Louis, the former is dated 16 November, 1979, while the latter, which went through four drafts, is dated February 1980. I think Dorn felt that the influence of Black Mountain poetry in England, particularly via Cambridge, was well covered here. This formed one of my areas of interest. Clark says:

> I went to Gonville and Caius College... because of Donald Davie's presence there... and I [also] studied Verse Tragedy with Jeremy Prynne... [who] had the best library I'd ever seen of the poetry we're talking about—Black Mountain specifically. ... [O]f course he had Olson, and was in the process of working on Olson's papers. And he had your [Dorn's] books....
>
> Donald Davie... was a sucker for you [Dorn], liked your work immediately, fell for the landscape and the sense of place and the nostalgia, the wistful qualities. Something must have been touched in him. Jeremy was seeing the work in terms of a literary movement with which he was familiar, but I think Davie was seeing it in more traditional emotional terms, landscape, Wordsworth. He was interested in a syntax that somehow in poetry carries the feeling along in an undiscursive way, that the emotions are displayed by the small movements you do inside the syntax.
>
> And then of course there was Andrew Crozier... [who] wanted to explain certain Black Mountain poetry as in the English lyrical tradition, as a development from Early Renaissance lyricism—which in fact it was.
>
> None of these guys had any idea of what American speech was about, however. A number of the moves that you and others were making were passing them by in the dark.[7]

---

[7] *Little Caesar*, 11 (1981), 192-4.

Clark goes on to distinguish between two main approaches in contemporary American poetry:

> [In the case of] Black Mountain, I look at every writer there as having gone through a process that is one of the main things you've got to learn about writing, that is, how to incorporate the social experience into words. Whereas in the St. Marks scene, in keeping with the whole tradition that Allen [Ginsberg]'s talking about of Rimbaud and Artaud and everything else, it was the high of the strictly personal experience. This also includes the experience of *personality*, which of course is what this type of poet is supposed to become.[8]

Clark briefly discusses his time at Essex University, including his editing and production of the mimeograph *Once, Twice, Thrice* (etc) and Davie's disappointment with his seemingly Bohemian progress. Here there is considerable overlap with the proposed continuation of my own interview.[9]

Since some of the remarks made at the two 1981 readings might, with Dorn's permission and due rearrangement, have found their way into the interview book, I'll provide a few extracts below.

---

[8] ibid, 208.
[9] Some sense of how Dorn's and Davie's interests may have intersected can be gleaned from the latter's *A Travelling Man—Eighteenth Century Bearings* (Carcanet Press, 2002), the introduction to which (by Doreen Davie) stresses the author's Dissenter background and his appreciation of "how scientific language could serve poetry's purposes". This also includes passages from Davie's journal which cover the period at Essex University. Despite their falling out over the revolt at Essex, Davie continued to acknowledge the strength of Dorn's work: "I believe your life, private as well as public, has gone disastrously wrong since we were in Dromahair [in August] last year... [yet] the poetry you've been writing [i.e. that later published as *Twenty-four Love Songs*] is as beautiful as ever—much more so than *The North Atlantic Turbine*." (Davie to Dorn, 28 May 1968, Box 8, Folder 87, Dorn Papers, U Conn).

Introducing *Recollections of Gran Apachería* the poet said:

> [This work] comes out of a ... preoccupation with the American South-West, more from the standpoint of looking across the border, south to north. It was the result of a course I was doing at Kent State in the early '70s—a class that actually got me in on it, [including] people from the present rock group Devo. There are a series of portraits that begin with miniature Apache figures. It's meant to be a very distant look, I hope. I mean [if] that sounds uninvolved and cold, then from my standpoint that's good. The history of the so-called white man's involvement with the so-called red man is too obviously psychotic and complicated for any other method to be in operation really. In this case the way the book was laid out and printed: the first lines not as any kind of pretension that they were significant or meant anything themselves but more for their kind of choate effects.[10] [Reads 'First Lines' down to the line "Captain Emmet Crawford".] That pretty much runs through what I'm calling a little portrait part. After that [i.e. 'A Period Portrait of Sympathy'] the book becomes quite strongly opinionated and that's another part of it.[11]

One of my extra questions concerned the transition from this denser kind of text to spontaneous shorter pieces:

> I didn't buy *Hello, La Jolla* when it came out. It was wrapped in cellophane and I couldn't look inside; then someone let me have a peek and I felt the material was lightweight. Silly because a lot of the British poetry I like is brief, not massive. Then Asa Benveniste told me he found it more interesting than your earlier verse and I went out and bought a copy.

---

[10] At the East West Gallery, 1995, Dorn stated with greater clarity: "Suddenly I realized that the first lines of the poems were making a kind of thematic string through the work, so I printed those up front." Private recording.

[11] Dorn, Reading at the Poetry Society, London, 19 June 1981, private recording.

Now I'm convinced of its value but I'd be interested to find out how you came to that mode.

Dorn had already commented helpfully on this:

> That [*Recollections of Gran Apachería*] was my way of keeping myself on my feet while I struggled with the undeniable fact that I was going to have to write Book IIII of *Gunslinger*, and about the same time I started keeping a notebook on the problems of California, both "No Cal" and "So Cal". All of that resulted in *Hello, La Jolla*.[12] I had been commuting from San Francisco to San Diego once a week and I couldn't quite bring myself to move there. That was the heyday of PSA [Pacific Southwest Airlines]—$28 round trip to San Diego[13]—and, although the book bears that title and in some ways is about So Cal phenomenology, it's really more ambitious than that conceptually—although it's nothing much in terms of length and large scale attack. It starts with one thing I'm interested in, which is sort of a direct resurrection of Modern aphoristic statement. It has a preface which is meant to be a kind of coda: "These dispatches should be/received in the spirit/of the Pony Express:/light and essential." ... And there are certain attempts to get widespread ironies at work in it [as with] this quote from a man named John L. Stoddard, ... who was a famous lecturer before the media killed off his type. [Reads quotation.] Obviously he was no prophet! But it's nice to remember that in fact one's initial impression of California in the old days was that it was a kind of paradise.

---

[12] Jennifer Dunbar Dorn comments: "Ed taught at UC San Diego during winter, 1976. The poems for both books [*Hello, La Jolla* and *Yellow Lola*] were written 1976–78" (email, 27 February 2011). Since the material was arranged and published 1978–80 it could be treated as late '70s work.

[13] At his reading at the Institute of United States Studies, Dorn refers to the midnight PSA flight between San Francisco and LA, "a dangerous trip to take because of the weirdos on it, but you can still do it."

> This book [*Hello, La Jolla*] is quite dated in some respects—not a quality which bothers me a lot.... An example of that [is] 'What Will Be Historically Durable'.... Then there's a section called *Flywheel Programs*, which is meant to [suggest] what I take it the function of aphorism is: which is be consequential in itself to the extent that it's supposed to have a kind of recovery in the mind that goes on and on—that's what the reason for the form is based on.... All this... sort of dovetails into Book II of *Hello, La Jolla*, which is *Yellow Lola*.[14]

At the same reading, Dorn elaborates on this in responding to a member of the audience who asks, "Why do you settle for aphorism?":

> I think it's quite an honourable, though not practised, form—you have to be nineteenth century and French to qualify yourself by that, but... I got fascinated by the terms of flywheel programs in the sense that: it's dangerous now to appear wise and probably foolhardy as well, but on the other hand there is a form of writing which doesn't run on endlessly about what you think or what you think you know. Actually the only kind of poetry that I really am interested in seeing resurrected—because it's so in abeyance—is narrative, because I think it's what this age needs to reconstitute a sense of poetry at all. But in the meantime, since that doesn't seem to be a rapidly growing movement, perhaps aphoristic procedures can have a place. If you try to do that, to form a really good aphorism, the whole point of an aphorism is that it implies the rest of the story; in fact it's a critique of the idea that you need to know the rest of the story.... We've got this guy in the States called Paul Harvey. He begins a story. Then there's usually a long ad and when he comes on again he says, "And now, the rest of the story."

---

[14] Dorn, Reading at the Poetry Society, London, 19 June 1981, private recording.

It's never a story, it's just some anecdote.[15]

Dorn describes the second volume as pieces of rock "picked out with tweezers" by Tom Clark:

> [*Yellow Lola*] comes out of *Hello, La Jolla*. It's just matter taken from my notebook. I didn't actually see it as a book till Tom Clark came along and said, "This is a book too, so why not be honest?"[16]
>
> He gave it the title 'Yellow Lola' and I gave it the subtitle 'formerly titled Japanese Neon', which is of course a lie—it was never.[17]

Dorn refers to it in his 19 June 1981 reading as "an elegant little book" with its Hockney cover image, and he is candid about the Californian publishing scene, Jeffrey Miller (Cadmus Editions) being an "acolyte" of John Martin (Black Sparrow Press), one of whose boasts is "that he never pays the writer".

Occasional remarks shed light on the larger process. Introducing '101' (*Yellow Lola*, 25) at the same reading, Dorn observes that this highway, which runs from Seattle to San Diego, is "a sea road surrounded by parallels". Beyond the literal, geographical context for pieces scrawled while driving, this gives philosophical weight to a text such as "The poet must always/be loyal to the poem/no matter what/other forms may beckon" ('101', *Yellow Lola*, 84). The travel mode becomes, in both books, an emblem of Californian existence, a culture once sought as a paradise by dust-swept

---

[15] And in a twist that would surely have appealed to Dorn, FBI files released under the Freedom of Information Act revealed that Harvey "enjoyed a 20-year friendship with J. Edgar Hoover, often submitting advance copies of his radio script for comment and approval" (CBS News report, 22 January 2010).

[16] "Tom Clark... moved to Boulder in 1980" (Jennifer Dunbar Dorn, email, 27 Feb, 2011). Hence the two writers were in close proximity at this stage.

[17] Dorn, Reading at the Poetry Society, London, 19 June 1981, private recording.

pioneers and now, for both inhabitants and visitors, a condition of restlessness amid mocked-up beauty. Differently from Steinbeck's depiction of illusory manna or Ginsberg's indignation in *Thru the Vortex West Coast to East*, Dorn probes the terminology of a suspiciously lulling dream, drawing force from the inconsequential. His take on dystopia—circa 1980—is more *Brave New World* than *Nineteen Eighty-Four*.

Dorn's links with English counter-culture are indicated in his account of 'The Metric System' (*Yellow Lola*, 36):

> That's a kind of bow to John Michell, an English writer [who] I value very much because of his radical traditionalist pamphlets on Babylon and measure/metrication,[18] plus several other books—*The Flying Saucer Vision*, for instance.[19]

At a play level, this might appear one more instance of wackiness, English laid against Californian, but Michell's heretical theory adds to the critique of disembodiment. As Dorn subsequently stated, "because of the extreme brevity of its components", *Yellow Lola* "gets its effect cumulatively".[20]

Dorn's sardonic wit allows no refuge in standard liberal postures. While exposing corporate greed and government malpractice, he is still able to detect ironies, and a certain relativity, within this exercise of power. Asked "How did Nixon rob the Post Office?" (see 'What Will Be Historically Durable', *Hello, La Jolla*, 19), Dorn explains at his 19 June 1981 reading:

---

[18] See particularly, *A Defence of Sacred Measures* (Cokaygne, 1972). Michell's other major works are *The View Over Atlantis* and *City of Revelation*. A long-term resident of Notting Hill, he was involved with the London Free School in the mid-1960s.

[19] Dorn, Reading at the Institute of United States Studies, London, 16 June 1981, private recording.

[20] Interview with Tandy Sturgeon (1984) in *Ed Dorn Live: Lectures, Interviews and Outtakes*, ed. Joseph Richey (University of Michigan Press, 2007), 50.

He made it into a semi-private corporation again. Because the Post Office has always lost money, which is presumably what the Post Office is supposed to do if the service is good. In a way he's pre-Reaganite, although with hindsight he's not nearly so bad—it almost looks like a Golden Age. Nevertheless, one of his big acts was to take the Post Office out of federal hands and put it on a paying basis, which meant of course that the service fell off and the price went up— which is what private enterprise always does. So even Nixon has his due—it's ironic in a sense. That's just a commentary on how Americans can be suckered really.

I am struck by how topical such remarks remain, as the threatened privatization of Royal Mail looms closer.

Dorn's preamble for a still uncollected poem suggests a transition from the *Hello, La Jolla/Yellow Lola* phase to the broader political thrust of *Abhorrences*.[21] A significant historical moment is registered through tiny detail, allowing bathos to sharpen into taut critique, with an aphoristic resonance in the last line. 19 June 1981:

I'm going to do an isolated poem or piece, which I almost never do. I did [this] a few weeks back right out of the newspaper.[22] It's sort of a gesture to the movement of certain figures looming large on the American political landscape— like, one is Alexander the Haigiographer.[23] This particular

---

[21] Introducing *Abhorrences* at the East West Gallery in 1995, Dorn said: "I never got much interested in whether they're poems or not... they look like poems, they're optically poems.... Mainly they're very short essays, setting forth various pieces of impatience.... The opening onslaught is a... summary of a certain kind of vocabulary that was active during [the 1980s] in America, which is a place that has a mania for the stupidest form of euphemism you can possibly come up with."

[22] This second sentence is interpolated from the 16 June reading.

[23] This word sounds more like "hemiographer" or "heliographer" but, allowing for tape distortion from the acoustic of a large room, I have plumped for a play on Haig's name which recalls his verbal habits (circumlocution or mixed metaphor) and self-importance. Following the Reagan assassi-

guy happens to be Caspar Weinberger, the Permanent Secretary of Defense, the Secretary of Defense being what in an honester age was called the Secretary of War. In the nineteenth century. There were some great Secretaries of War, actually. Caspar Weinberger is no such thing. I mean a government run by businessmen cannot produce great [statesmen]. It's called 'How Small Can Awesome Get?'

Dorn had revised the poem (initially called 'Personage') since writing it in Boulder on 19 April 1981.[24] 'How Small Can Awesome Get'/'Personage', and two other contemporaneous uncollected poems, are printed in this volume, following 'The Riverside Interview'.

There is insufficient space here to reproduce Dorn's comments, at both readings, about the recently composed *Captain Jack's Chaps*, but the following statement from 19 June 1981 is worth quoting for its general application: "Since I don't write poems really so much as books it's difficult to read any one [portion]."

Again, there is stress on a developing weave: the habit of sustained but free trial associated with Black Mountain. Dorn has acknowledged how Olson generated "an expansionary force".[25] A parallel can be made too with Prynne's structures, both at the

---

nation attempt on March 30th, Haig had aroused controversy and ridicule for his comment that he was "in control here", against what is laid down in the constitution. This would form part of the cultural/historical background to Dorn's statement.

[24] The original version survives in a notebook, called *The Joy of Nothing/by no one*, its main title deriving from the brand name, with author tag added in Dorn's hand (Box 42, Dorn Papers, UConn). Used over the period 1981–93, this contains, among other things, a text of *Captain Jack's Chaps* dated December 1981. The original refers to the "threshold of Germany", rather than Bonn airport, "the symbolic touching" of the tie knot, and "the quality" rather than "the signal". A minute topicality is retained in the honing process. Weinberger left the USA for London on 4 April 1981 and was in Bonn for a NATO meeting on 7 April. The earlier title suggests, ironically, a person of note; also perhaps, a guise, an assumed role of office. The later version was published in *Spectacular Diseases*, 6, ed. Robert Vas Dias (1981).

[25] 'From Imperial Chicago', in *Ed Dorn Live*, 58.

macro-level of a book such as *Brass* and the micro-level of a poem like 'For This, For This' (with its interleaving of passages from *The Cell of Self-Knowledge*). In a late 1970s/early '80s context, it is interesting to compare *Down Where Changed* with Dorn's short-cumulative takes on the Western political-economic scene. Each writer has moved from a more overt focus on landscape to oblique consideration of cultural space, retaining the concern with "exchange" which Ian Brinton has noted.[26] Formally, this involves a series of page-pieces that possess a kind of concentrated casualness, although Prynne's procedures are more rigorously patterned, with much use of the three-line stanza (mathematical as stock, one might say). Dorn's pieces, of course, are separately titled and not so obviously on-going. But whatever the difference in weight—some readers would prefer Prynne's response to "the lurid airways"—there is a common deployment of discrete but related units.

Too often perhaps, when considering influence within a literary circle, we focus on similarities rather than difference. Once shared ground is established, it is more crucial to notice points of divergence. This is applicable to the way in which Dorn and then Prynne branched out from Olson, with particularities of attention and sound. It pertains also to Raworth's development: the forging of "continuous" syntax, as Dorn calls it, with "intellectual" as opposed to "syntactical leaps".[27] There is a strong London component in this, despite American and Essex/Cambridge links. That said, Raworth's *Writing* (1975–77: published 1982) could be read alongside coeval work by the other poets as another serial form of language pressure. Raworth's earlier "distrust of massiveness", as Geoffrey Ward terms it,[28] which led to a preference for snapshot process, has given way to a method of combining longer reach with the atomized unit. The ex-telephone operator and film-watcher

---

[26] 'his brilliant luminous shade', in *A Manner of Utterance: The Poetry of J.H. Prynne*, ed. Ian Brinton (Shearsman Books, 2009), 20-1.

[27] 'Abhorrences concerning the State of American Poetry', in *Ed Dorn Live*, 43.

[28] 'On Tom Raworth', in *Perfect Bound* (Winter 1976/7), 14.

comes back, in split-continuity, with a work for "the moles and the bats".[29]

With regard to a long poem such as *Gunslinger*, Dorn remarked in 1973 that he establishes

> a way of speaking that tends to rule what I say, because I'm anxious to keep a rhetorical tension there. So the poem doesn't break… or, if it is falling apart, [to make clear] that it's supposed to.[30]

Ward acknowledges this "continuity of voice," while arguing that it "leaves Dorn free from obligations to systematize his material" until a late stage. He argues that in this work the "procedures of each book differ; the first contains no blueprint for the last."[31] *Gunslinger* clearly marks a shift in the use and arrangement of material. Much earlier, "things like [Robert Duncan's] *The Venice Poem*" showed Dorn how "you could organize thought into a long, sustained and fairly ordered structure."[32] Later, his stay in England freed him up from the kind of poetics embodied in *Geography*, so that language didn't have to carry such a moral burden.[33] Raworth might be an influence here, encouraging a less programmatic mode as well as a different kind of expression. Yet the variousness or contingency of things found "on the air"[34] does not dispel a relational instinct.

Perhaps the most interesting part of my interview concerns the (then unfashionable) relevance of pre-Romantic literature to Dorn and the 1960–80s period. I had studied Swift, Pope,

---

[29] *Writing* (The Figures, 1982), title page.
[30] 'An Interview with Roy K. Okada', *Interviews* ed. Donald Allen (Four Seasons Foundation, 1980), 56.
[31] 'Gunslinger IIII', in *Perfect Bound* (Summer 1976), 74.
[32] John Wright, 'An Interview with Edward Dorn' [4 September, 1990], *Chicago Review* 39: 1 (1993); reprinted in *Edward Dorn, American Heretic/Chicago Review* 49: 3 & 50: 1 (Summer 2004), 174.
[33] ibid, 206-7.
[34] 'Road-Testing the Language', *Interviews*, 103.

Johnson and Byron in some depth, and was now getting interested in Charles Churchill, all of which dovetailed with a knowledge of Renaissance satire, especially Marston's work. Dorn's manoeuvres in the spirit of eighteenth century satire were so different from, say, Peter Porter's, and I was keen to investigate a procedure that was simultaneously loose and formal. We didn't get far on this occasion but the "stub" interview shows how advantageous it was for Dorn, with his midwestern roots, to encounter parts of a British writing tradition *in situ*, indeed at a point, the 1960s, when this older cultural order was in flux. Clark's remarks about Black Mountain and the Renaissance lyric, quoted above, are also relevant here. Despite Dorn's anxieties about an alien take on English life, he was by friendship, work, and his second marriage, brought into fruitful familiarity with what might otherwise have remained remote. *Rolling Stock*, with Jennifer at the helm, can be seen as a fusion of American and British traditions of underground journalism.[35] By the early '80s a different kind of radical resistance was evident, and Dorn tapped into this, at a contemporary and historical level.[36] As

---

[35] I refer to a lively pamphlet and magazine culture which goes back to the seventeenth century. Specifically, however, in the 1966–76 period, there were close ties between US, Canadian and British alternative newspapers, sometimes literally in terms of content and contributors but otherwise in a context of shared aims/influences. Dorn expresses some surprise that Iain Sinclair saw copies of the Writing Supplement to *Georgia Straight* 8 (27 July 1971), in which Dorn and Prynne had editorial input (*Ed Dorn Live*, 161). If it is any further gauge, I read the Vancouver newspaper during this period, alongside British equivalents. For the underground newspaper scene in London, see *The Riverside Interviews 6: Tom McGrath* and Nigel Fountain, *Underground: the London Alternative Press 1966–74* (Comedia/Routledge, 1988).

[36] Parallels, in less overt form, may be found in Prynne's work. As N.H. Reeve and Richard Kerridge observe: "There is a good deal of abrasive sarcasm, particularly in the first half of *The Oval Window* [which] appeared in 1983, and has a specifically early-1980s British political edge to it, with the persistent tones of free-market cynicism and the use of highly-charged phrases like "safe in our hands"… [S]uch fleeting allusions… are like guerrilla raids on the euphemistic manipulations of the day" (*Nearly Too Much: The Poetry of J.H. Prynne* [Liverpool University Press, 1995], 175). The clown Lavatch's words from *All's Well*

repression hit with a sweep scarcely imagined at Grosvenor Square in 1968, perhaps the only valid artistic reaction was a prismatic narrowing of the absurdity strung across the columns of *Bean News* (1972–74). The time required a chronicle that was more "surface-underground".

If Ginsberg's and Duncan's response to tyranny is essentially Blakean (in visionary spirit), Dorn's mode is more characteristically Swiftian—with the proviso that he must have relished Blake's satiric squibs. This is a matter of language and perspective, rather than allegiance. As Donald Wesling remarks, Dorn, in his circular (as opposed to top-centre) scan, "affiliates with the *mobile vulgus*."[37] The line of a language fitted for disturbance is traced in a relevant way by Pat Rogers:

> The vocabulary of Augustan satire… carries within itself a buried layer of allusion to civil unrest. The "premonition" is imagistic and rhetorical rather than literal; but it is still true that this body of writing prefigures an important development in populist activity, indeed in social history at large. The Scriblerian lexicon anticipated events.[38]

While, as he insists, not using such literature as a model, Dorn got inspiration from its sounds and procedures. The use of the explicatory or ironically counter-charged footnote in Swift and Pope seems to have offered possibilities for deployment in a late 1970s context. Some of the zanier devices in *Gunslinger* may also reflect an awareness of eighteenth century practice, as cartoon culture jostles with philosophy. Dorn's statements about aphorism, Classically derived, could be applicable to his radical inversion of the Western genre as well as to the later Californian work.

That Ends Well provide an oblique perspective on such corruption.

[37] "'To fire we give everything": Dorn's Shorter Poems', in *Internal Resistances: the Poetry of Edward Dorn,* ed. Donald Wesling (University of California Press, 1985), 15.

[38] *Hacks and Dunces: Pope, Swift and Grub Street* (Methuen, 1980), 114.

Rather as the Punk moment drew partly on an older Notting Hill counter-culture, a confluence of energies is apparent in Dorn's 1981 stance. The cynical Midwesterner, the survivor of radical experiment, brings authority of reading to explode lazy thought and blind obedience. With consciousness dipped in the first Reagan landscape, he is equipped to analyse and record the larger manoeuvres of empire. As I have indicated, the groundwork for *Abhorrences* is being laid, by transition from the two books of epigrams: (mostly) single day or month annotation of the processes of a decade.[39] These works are paradoxically outside or beyond the self and absolutely tied to the circumstance of perception. They inhabit their time, embody an era in language current.

Dorn's last major work, *Languedoc Variorum*, returns to a larger pre-1977 scale, mimicking the layered texture of scholarly editions for fierce, playful inquiry. Each page juxtaposes text (overtly poetic), subtexts and nazdaks (more prose-textured), the last, in Herbie Butterfield's description, a kind of "telegrammese".[40] This procedure, with the bottom level as a parody of breaking news, recalls, as I have suggested, eighteenth century practice. There are more ancient precedents, including illuminated manuscripts, but the graft of pamphlet and compendium in the period from, say, Swift to Byron, provides particularly fruitful examples of "built-in" deconstruction. So the 1990s are refracted via a Scriblerian travail/pilgrimage to the Medieval. As Dorn explained in 1997, heresy becomes "a metaphor for... oppressive and corruptive control

---

[39] It could be argued that Dorn's epigrammatic/aphoristic style emerges earlier, from his keeping of a daybook in 1971 (entitled *The Day & Night Report*). Some of this was published in, among other places, the Writing Supplement of *Georgia Straight* (no: 8, 27 July, 1971). Dorn's reading at the A Space Gallery, Toronto, 2 February 1973, also includes a number of very short poems.

[40] 'Ed(ward Merton) Dorn... A Memoir, an Introduction, An Overview, Some Poems, and a Song', Essex University commemorative talk, April 2000; published in *Cento Magazine* (http://epc.buffalo.edu/authors/dorn/DORN_CENTO/dorn_cento_index.html).

[by the state]."[41] *Languedoc Variorum* has the cinematic and pulp elements of *Gunslinger*, the territorial sweep of 'Idaho Out', but also the severity of *Abhorrences*. Dorn's cankered muse joins with the font of song (Pound being an obvious reference point here). With hindsight the 1981 interview and readings foreshadow that final balance of play and protestant dissent.

To assert these continuities is not to overlook the variousness of Dorn's work. Accordingly, this volume includes two chapters from *Juneau in June*, a work that was never finished or published or collected. In the summer of 1980 Dorn had a teaching job at the University of Alaska "which entailed workshops with prisoners in Juneau and many trips by plane and ferry to various campuses in Sitka, Skagway, etc."[42] The travel book or journal deals with the contradictions of a right wing libertarian state, its contemporary make-up and geographical-historical features ("Up here latitude is everything"). Introducing a second chapter, 'Alaska Loca', Dorn remarked at his 16 June 1981 reading:

> The Alaska Prison system is an actual extension of the University of Alaska, so that in a sense when you're in prison you're on the campus of the university. That may say something about their attitude to universities. I didn't inquire much about that.

Juneau in June draws partly on the voices of prisoners; indeed the epigraph to this other chapter is described as "a rap, because that's what happens in prison all the time." This kind of work, closer to journalism, is witty in a freer, more relaxed way than some of the poetry projects; see, for instance, the earlier piece, '*ALASKA*: in Two Parts', from *Hello, La Jolla*. Reading from the travel book in the summer of 1981, Dorn had his listeners in stitches, and the recording which survives is a good reminder of his skill as an

---
[41] 'The Protestant Ethic Revisited', in *Ed Dorn Live*, 136.
[42] Jennifer Dunbar Dorn, email, 5 November, 2010.

entertainer.⁴³ But ultimately we come back, as Olson said, "to the geography of it"⁴⁴—a shape of voice or voices in the land.

Finally, in a London context, I had planned to inquire about the genesis of *Manchester Square*, the sequence written in collaboration with Jennifer Dunbar.⁴⁵ A letter from Dorn to Robert Vas Dias, who requested work for book publication, implies that this provided the stimulus to shape and complete a work-in-progress:

> ...it occurs to me that from your asking simply for a book has come a bite you might not be ready to chew. I got really interested once the idea soaked in and saw it as a report to the nation, or at least a little guide to W1 from both of us, as guests of the winter, and intimately entwined. (1 July 1975)

Reminiscing, Jennifer Dunbar Dorn says:

> 'Home again' looks like a collaboration, for instance— mostly mine but with some Ed touches. 'Manchester Square' and 'St. Christopher's Place' are mine, but the others are Ed's or his with some input from me. [During our stay in England] 1974–75, Ed taught a couple of days a week at U of Essex. We lived at Bentinck St during Autumn term (I taught at Balham School for boys, Kidd went to school at St. Georges Hanover Square) and then spent Spring term in Cambridge.⁴⁶

To separate the strands somewhat in this way is not to negate overall unity; the writing displays a shared impulse throughout.

---

⁴³ Dorn had read similar extracts to a quieter audience, it seems, at Buffalo on 24 March, 1981. At that point, the text of the first chapter was less fully formed; it is considerably shorter but contains one paragraph (after "sleep promoting matter.") that does not appear in the London text.

⁴⁴ 'Maximus to Gloucester, Letter 27 [withheld]', in *The Maximus Poems*, ed. G. Butterick (University of California Press, 1983), 184.

⁴⁵ Published by Permanent Press (London), December 1975.

⁴⁶ Email, 22 February, 2011.

As appropriate to an area which combines pulsing business with calmer life, and sophistication with grosser features, the book has both lyric grace and a sharp registration of behaviour. Among its evocative images are the "lone over-bred Daimler/weak in the front quarters/a strong, rather literal trunk" ('Grosvenor Square') and the older pieces "blown away,/like the eyes of Selfridges" ('Manchester Square').

Although there is some overlap with Dorn's Californian texts (for instance, the dog excreta in 'Mount Street'), this sequence has a more sustained concentration and integrated form. Any socio-political critique is implicit rather than overt, as with the description of the bronze eagle on the US embassy in Grosvenor Square. The residual irony of a woman "dying on the cobblestones" in an alley of smart shops is treated with emotional tact ('St. Christopher's Place'). As Edward Powell notes, these poems have an "accumulation of mood and fact" simply and directly conveyed.[47] The urban scene is analysed anthropologically ("The deeper mysteries of the body repose in fur") and described by gut response: "I have a nervousness/alternating between the rude traffic/and the potential/but only reputational crossfire"—this as the child Kid runs ahead, close to a pair of officials ('Carlos Place').[48] The penultimate poem is a little note to "Herbie" (Butterfield), which evokes a Williams idiom. It is good to be reminded of the warmth of which Dorn was capable, given appropriate conditions.

The issue of collaboration brings back Dorn's acknowledged debt to friends and mentors such as Prynne and Raworth. It is interesting to note how his comments in the 1981 interview echo those made four months earlier in a Charles Olson Memorial Lecture at SUNY, Buffalo.[49] Any text comes out of "a complex of

---

[47] 'Selected Books', *Oasis*, 16 (1976), 64.
[48] If not coincidental, there may be a background allusion to the terrorist Carlos Sanchez here. Paris police identified him as a suspect in June 1975.
[49] 'The Real Effect of Affect and Applicability', 24 March, 1981. Recording available online at Pennsound. In the talk which preceded this on 19

occasions", to borrow Olson's phrase.⁵⁰ Dorn's melodic and mental acuteness reflects a dialogue with writers of affinity or occasional opposition, past and present.⁵¹

March, Dorn refers to Olson's role as pedagogue, "a word he spoke honouring its history, not its present perjorative use."
⁵⁰ 'Maximus to Gloucester, Letter 27 [withheld]'; *The Maximus Poems*, 185.
⁵¹ Dorn's modesty and tact with regard to his own contribution means that we must draw on the word of others. Tom Raworth, for instance, says that *A Serial Biography* "probably wouldn't have been written without the encouragement of Tom [Clark] and Ed" (*Vort*, 1 [Fall 1972], 33). A proper account of Dorn's influence upon Prynne still needs to be written. The ties go deep, involving regular correspondence and encounters at crucial points. To risk a tabloid-type detail, *Kitchen Poems* was apparently so-named—at a literal level at least—because its contents were written in the Dorns' house in Colchester. Ease of manner is qualified by or charged with a sort of electric buzz—the tenor of the time but also a way of reading/seeing carried from Black Mountain. The shaping of a mode of inquiry which retains a strong lyric element, and the juxtaposition of technical with homely or street language, seem to reflect something of Dorn's practice. Beneath the tighter impress of Prynnean discourse we may partly glimpse the American's "rangy, gestural, highly individualized syntax", as Tom Clark calls it (*Edward Dorn: A World of Difference* [North Atlantic Books, 2002], 13). As argued above, the measure of influence here is not sameness but particularity which stems from another('s) affect. The influence the other way, particularly upon *Gunslinger*, with its increasingly "inner" field of reference, also deserves investigation.

THE RIVERSIDE INTERVIEW

Edward Dorn interviewed by Gavin Selerie

London, July 1981

Opposite: Edward Dorn at the Poetry Society / National Poetry Centre, Earl's Court, London, June 1981; photograph by Alan Burgis; courtesy of Gavin Selerie.

SELERIE: First of all I'd like to talk to you about your time at Essex. I gather you were visiting professor there—was that the title?—from 1965 to 1968.

DORN: Technically, for the first two years—from Autumn of 1965 to 1967, I was a Fulbright lecturer; that was the source of the funding. Then I worked for the university directly the following year, went back to the United States and did a term at the University of Kansas at Lawrence, and finally returned to the University of Essex for the '69/'70 academic year. But I suppose the general title would have been visiting professor. I came by the Fulbright lectureship through the agency of Donald Davie who requested that I be part of the programme he had designed for the Literature Department at Essex, the first academic year of which, I think, was 1964. I arrived in '65. Davie had come from Cambridge, bringing with him Tom Clark, Andrew Crozier, and John Barrell (who's now at Cambridge again). It was one of the most interesting, even perhaps brilliant, and certainly one of the oddest departments of literature ever concocted anywhere. It stayed together pretty well until the troubles which hit Essex in late '67 and '68.

SELERIE: And that clash between students and authority finally caused Davie to leave England?

DORN: I suppose you could say "caused him to", although I think in that case causes would be hard to ascribe. It was a general dissatisfaction and distaste with what I think he took to be cowardice on the part of his colleagues.

SELERIE: So it was dissatisfaction with the department rather than with the student body?

DORN: Well, I think it was a dissatisfaction with what he saw as the compliance of most of the faculty with the reigning student demands, which he thought should be resisted or at least mediated in a sharper way. I don't know the English academic structure that well but it seems to me that the post he had, that of Pro-Vice-Chancellor, put him in a scapegoat position if anything went down. I think he bore the brunt, perhaps unfairly, of a lot of issues that on the one hand he didn't create and on the other hand he was really not able to resolve. Nor would anyone have been. If you're in a position such as that and you suffer for a situation which is not of your personal doing, there's a certain amount of legitimate paranoia that is generated out of that. And certainly he felt that.

SELERIE: How did the department at Essex differ from those in which you had taught before? You taught at Idaho State I think, which presumably was a pretty conservative institution.

DORN: Idaho State was conservative in the sense that it was a typical state college that had suddenly been turned into a university—on paper. I mean one day it had been called Idaho State College and then the next day it was called Idaho State University, and nothing really changed. It was a fairly conscientious little university in the sticks in a kind of cowboy state, and very much under the pressure and restrictions of a large Mormon population. A lot of the students were Mormons. So going from there to Essex was a very big jump indeed. There was a certain kind of intellection at the University of Essex that didn't prevail at all at Idaho—as an institution. Obviously there were very good people at Idaho State and I probably knew most of them; nevertheless, there was little to compare with the general atmosphere and excitement of a new university in those days. After all, it wasn't just the department of Literature at Essex; it was Sociology and Political Science, with people like Alasdair MacIntyre who I think was a reformed theologian. It was a group of highly enterprising characters.

SELERIE: Was the university set up along inter-disciplinary lines, as at Sussex?

DORN: The scheme there, which I think still prevails to a certain extent, is... When in the recent cuts, for instance, small Russian departments around the country were snipped because too few students were doing the subject, Essex escaped because such languages and concentrations of language were tied to the study of literature. That was the ideal; I suppose you could call it interdisciplinary.

SELERIE: That was rather like Black Mountain, wasn't it?—to put Literature, or the Arts perhaps, at the core of everything.

DORN: There was a certain similarity, yeah. Structurally, of course, there's not much similarity because the University of Essex was, and still is, a state university and is funded as such; whereas Black Mountain was a small private university—college actually—and it was always faced with money problems from beginning to end. It was quite small: Black Mountain never had more than about a hundred students ever and that was in its heyday; when it was sliding towards its end it had twenty-five or thirty students in fact. By contrast, Essex was and is a legitimate state university. But in spirit there would be quite a lot of connexion. The Language undergraduates did a four year course instead of the usual three year course, and they studied Spanish, Portuguese, Russian and American—which is a language the English presumably don't have to learn. It was in its time and in a way still is quite radical as an idea. It wasn't necessarily radical politically; the fact that it became so I think had more to do with the process by which the whole taste of the time became deeply radical, and that happened everywhere to a wide extent. But pedagogically it was radical.

SELERIE: What was your personal role within that framework?

DORN: I was there to teach American Literature, which I did through various things: the short story, a certain amount of poetry. One of the great satisfactions for me was that I had for four or five years been doing creative writing workshops as well as literature courses at Idaho, and Essex—to my great relief—demanded no such teaching of "creativity". One could really get down to hard information and transmit that, and I was excited to be given the chance to do this by Donald Davie. He generously provided the opportunity for me to work that way and in fact he suggested the direction I should take. It was really his idea that I do a course called 'The Literature of the Westward Expansion'; he felt that I could do that and naturally I was eager to construct a course along those lines. Davie was a great academic administrator actually—no doubt about it. As a writer and teacher I found that the Essex plan aided and abetted my own aims very much, because I was made to acquire the knowledge to do these things, instead of sitting with a bunch of potential writers and laboriously going over their work—which can be useful but it rarely is. It's much better to let people write and to convey other things to them which will enable them to write, rather than trying to tell them what they've written after they've done it.

SELERIE: So you leave them to go away and work things out for themselves.

DORN: Of course, in one sense, all students from the late sixties were brilliant compared with now. Perhaps not ultimately better but they certainly seemed to be better; there was an eagerness of acquisition that is not so evident these days.

SELERIE: An adventurousness. People would go off on their own and discover things in the library.

DORN: Yes, much more.

SELERIE: Can you give me an outline of the kind of authors that you suggested people should read?

DORN: Well, I did this for several years and, quite frankly, I began mainly with what I'd learned from Olson, who fed me a big bowl of oatmeal—to call that the sustenance of what I got at Black Mountain.

SELERIE: Are you talking about the materials on the American West as set out in the bibliography which he did for you?'

DORN: Yes. I tended to concentrate on Bernard DeVoto and his books, which are not complicated and are full of the enthusiasm of that field.

SELERIE: And Parkman?

DORN: Yes. I didn't so much concentrate on the archaeological aspect of Olson's bibliography because that kind of thing was harder to deal with at Essex, given the state of the library and so forth. Some of that material is just difficult to obtain, especially in a new university which starts out with a scanty library. So to a certain extent there were limitations. But after a while things improved because of the increasing use of photographic reproduction. People perhaps forget just how crucial that development was; the rise of Xerox freed a lot of knowledge that had previously only been available to specialists.

SELERIE: Jeremy Prynne's research work for other writers—or perhaps I should merely say communication of facts that he found interesting—is a prime example of this.

DORN: It is indeed. So through that agency it became possible to widen the latitude considerably. I was then able to go into more specific aspects of the American southwest and Indian culture. By the time I left the course was just getting designed; it was at that point when it could have become institutionalized as a section of the Literature course. It had taken me three years to work out what to do with that area of study and there had been a genuine excitement—shared by the students as well, I feel—in trying to discover what that course might be. Many of the students that I had there—and I've stayed in touch with a lot of them—still reflect the attitude of that kind of search that we made together. Nick Sedgwick, for instance, who's living down south of the river somewhere, went to Arizona and has written a fine book of poems which I saw recently. I can see in his work the influence of this particular approach to knowledge.

SELERIE: In *What I See in The Maximus Poems* you imply that what Olson taught you wasn't so much to do with content as with method—the way of approaching a subject. I take it that you meant digging deep within a particular field that you had discovered or chosen...

DORN: I think what Olson had in mind when he said method was something far more sophisticated than I ever meant, because for one thing his academic training was quite different from mine. But in so far as I could translate that method into discovery, I agree with you: it was a method. I never really had that much method in me; it's not my nature and it's not my background either. But sure, in any case some of that method in the way of seeing and the kind of desire to see would come out of what he was talking about as method. Yet in some ways I think Olson was a writer who had an eccentric take on scholarship and perhaps could have... For one thing, I don't think he was a scholar, as I've come to understand what that is. But he certainly was familiar with all the workings of scholarship and was very able in that discipline.

SELERIE: By saying that he was not a scholar do you mean that he was not living solely in the mind, not spending all his time in libraries, but was going out walking in the streets and listening to people talk rather than merely reading about them?

DORN: Indeed. I don't think he was narrow enough to be a scholar, and by that I don't mean anything limiting because I think the depth of scholarship is... it's not wide necessarily but it can be very penetrating. I don't think Olson knew anything with the kind of penetration that true scholarship involves; in other words, he had a kind of romantic idea about scholarship which I always loved actually. I think some of the people that he respected and admired were of this mould also: Waddell, for instance, was not a scholar, although he was a brilliant and speedy worker—he could assimilate vast areas very quickly and organize them in a new and interesting way.

SELERIE: 'All My Life I've Heard About Many.'

DORN: [laughs] But it's like a rocket, right? Whereas somebody like Denis O'Brien, for instance, at Cambridge, who knows Greek and wrote the Empedocles book which was such a hit in the late '60s, is a scholar.

SELERIE: But it would be impossible for a scholar—in that sense—to be a poet.

DORN: Well I don't know if I ever thought it would be, but—recently I've suddenly realized that it is entirely possible for a scholar to be a poet. Housman, for instance, whose collected classical reviews and monographs I've just acquired, was a great classical scholar and a poet.

SELERIE: But presumably his art depended upon him having sufficient leisure time to engage in his own activities. His small area of teaching and the rarified existence that a Cambridge professor had in those days enabled him to devote more time and energy to his writing than most university teachers could do now.

DORN: I think he chose to live in the university in a way that can still be defined as monastic. I'm told that he was the greatest classical scholar of his time, perhaps of any time, and he is also a great poet. I think this kind of monastic life, with no intrusion and consequently a totally controlled and sustained concentration, makes that possible. Olson, however, never had that situation. He was a man beset by the poverty that any writer might face. So it seems to me that circumstance dictates this a lot more than natural bent or ability. In this case I think circumstance really defines...

But of course this is not a comparison since Olson was obviously after a very different kind of registration of his sensibility. I don't think there are any kind of hierarchical judgements to be made here, but procedures do get defined by one's possibilities of living.

SELERIE: Can I go back a few years and ask you about the primary documents which you used for such narrative poems as 'Death While Journeying' and 'Ledyard'? I've been led by your poems to look at various books about the discovery of new territory in America and I wondered specifically what documents you used in writing about that phase of history.

DORN: Let's see. In a general sense I think Olson's bibliography, which was my teaching document at Black Mountain—I mean the document that he taught me with. That led me to Ledyard and that area of concern. I think it's possible to teach by bibliography but one has to qualify that immediately. If it's a place like Black Mountain and if it's a person like Olson who's using this method, that's one thing. Obviously, however, mere bibliographies are meaningless in other circumstances and I've seen people either in direct or indirect imitation of this method simply pile together a load of books. A list like that doesn't necessarily lead to anything. From this point of view, Olson's methodology was first rate. What that kind of method allows is that you're encouraged to follow your own taste with the teacher. But I saw very early on that if I considered this bibliography a kind of iron clad thing I had to do, then it would be useless. It was a document from which I could derive whatever I saw as meaningful for me at that point; it launched me on my own search for things. It was a loose guide to where I might explore, though it contained specific possibilities. There were certain parts of it that attracted me more than others, but then thinking about that was part of the education too. I don't mean to actually elevate my own articulation with this bibliography, but it seemed apparent to me that, if it were going to be a working instrument, I had to make my own use of it, which would be, as he would put it, "equal to his own". That was the way Olson had of speaking. So

I got interested in the historical part of that bibliography more than other parts, because for one thing when I was in the early part of my schooling I had more interest in geography and history than I did in archaeology, which still only interests me marginally because I don't have any archaeological experience. It strikes me that as an abstract interest it's not very useful. Certainly I've been around archaeologists and I've visited important sites, but in order to understand what's going on you would have to do some work with your hands in a particular place. In other words, that's the part of Olson's document that yields least to just reading.

SELERIE: Of course Olson himself did that in a minor way when he went to Yucatan.

DORN: That's right. I never did any of it, although I hung out with archaeologists; in fact, a great friend of mine, Max Pavesic, was the state archaeologist of the State of Idaho, and I got a lot of practical feel through him and from visiting sites. But not any direct experience; I never stayed at the camps for any length of time.

SELERIE: Does that have any impact on poems like 'The Land Below'—or is that composed mainly through a reading of Carl Sauer?

DORN: Well that's the geography-geology part. I suppose,—looking back on that poem, it strikes me as awfully off-the-wall and headstrong. I don't regret doing it but looking back on it I can see that I really barged in and made a lot of connexions that now I'd be more cautious about because I'm older and quite frankly I know more. But that was a time when I could take a certain kind of enthusiasm for things that I in fact in a couple of instances quoted and activate my own sense of aesthetic exploration of the mountains and the society that I lived in. Obviously a lot of that. Now we get into an aspect that really wasn't encouraged much in my time—although it's coming back to a slight extent—which is the narrative aspect of poetry. That was the first attempt to write a narrative poem in modern or—I can't stand the term "postmodern" but nevertheless that's what a lot of people call it—postmodern terms. I think actually that postmodern merely amounts to a more serious re-inspection of what has been taken as modern almost by rote. And in that sense *Idaho Out* is an early attempt to—

SELERIE: *Idaho Out*?

DORN: What were you referring to? Oh, 'The Land Below'. Both of those actually; in a way they're twin poems because *Idaho Out* was an Idaho version of what I'd attempted in New Mexico. They weren't that far apart. I went to Idaho from New Mexico so they were quite consecutive in that sense. I think 'The Land Below' was an attempt to do that on my own, just using the conventions of observation and narrative, whereas in *Idaho Out* I suppose I took a more serious look at what the content might include beyond that.

SELERIE: Going back to what you were saying about the innocent and zestful way that you went around looking at territory in those days, as opposed to the more rational and considered view that you might have now, it seems to me very valuable that you were able to go out and do that without worrying about total accuracy or consistency—the way you could bring a character like Boone into the poem at the end of the Meriwether Lewis thing. I don't know... if you'd taken a more structured, or I should say cautious, approach, perhaps it wouldn't have been so atmospheric. Perhaps you needed that directness, even if it wasn't—

DORN: Considered, in that sense—right, I agree, that's true. A poet's life, if it is a life, is of two kinds: it can be brilliant and short (there are a few examples of that and we all know them) or it can be long and laborious. Obviously mine wasn't brilliant and short. In fact, I started writing poetry after that would have been possible, even if I had been brilliant and short. Given this other approach, which clearly involves a longer life, I think the definition of a poet's life is really a life of study. And as that study progresses, the terms of its transmission change—not because the poetry changes but because the deliberation dictates what can be said. In this other category of what we would describe as a poet's life obviously the longer one is what I know; yet, having said that, you have to distinguish between approaches in any case. I believe that the whole function of poetry is the criticism of one's lifetime and one's life in that lifetime, and it's an endless attempt to encourage the reader to enlighten himself.

SELERIE: It seems to me particularly fruitful that you came to England when you did—in terms of what you've been talking about—because in the volume *Geography* you have some poems in which you're opening out the concern with the subjugation of the Red Man by the White Man, opening that out into a global examination of historical-geographical process. I'm thinking of such poems as 'Eugene Delacroix Says'. Then from that you move into the area indicated immediately in the title of the next book. I don't know exactly the circumstances of the composition of the poems in *The North Atlantic Turbine* but I assume that they were written after your arrival in Colchester.

DORN: Oh yes, they were.

SELERIE: So would it be true to say that your gradual widening of focus was brought about by the political ferment that was displayed in Europe and of course back home in America? The events which occurred in Berkeley in the mid-sixties must have provided material for commentary in a particularly direct way.

DORN: In fact I came here from Berkeley—from the poetry conference which has become a kind of touchstone for the mood of that time. Yes, for sure, it influenced the way that I was thinking and writing, although I think that should be revised from widening of focus, widening of field, to narrowing of field.

SELERIE: Because it becomes more political?

DORN: Yes. Well, I don't know if it becomes more political or not; certainly it becomes more concentrated in the sense that a beam from the sun goes through a glass and gets concentrated. The kind of wild, loose, broad-gauge scan that I was used to thinking in the States obviously didn't prevail here. The whole introduction to my ear of tone in the language and the resultant class definition that derives from that—all those things were new to me. Not just England but Europe in general definitely gave me another... I started all over in a sense and got a new hitch on the way I thought about things, in that it was always marvellous for me to hear the English speak in all their various tongues among themselves. You don't get that in the States at all; you get a kind of regional wiseness and a characteristic speech from various broad regions but you don't get actual tongues being articulated. You might but they're not used as definitions of persons really, except in the grossest sense; so that was all brand new. But the significant thing is that the people who have been important to me on this side—after Olson—are about the same number in such a small country as there have been in America. For instance, although I was older than Jeremy Prynne and in a certain way more determined in my objectives at that time, he nevertheless had studied far more deeply many things that I was curious about than I ever had—and that in fact I ever will. So I have no hesitation in saying that he was really my second teacher—quite definitely after Olson—and in a way that Olson never was. He fed me materials in a very generous way, in a prompting way at times, during the period when I was writing there. *Gunslinger*, for instance, bears the mark of his having introduced me to *Nature* magazine.

SELERIE: What about Parmenides?

DORN: I don't know whether he put me on to that directly or not—because actually it would be hard to pinpoint any of this. What I'm trying to say rather is that he introduced me to a more finite way of approaching the acquisition of knowledge than Olson, because Olson was always very wide-spread and wanted to take everything in a gulp, whereas Jeremy is very particular.

SELERIE: That is so of British culture in general. We've got a great ability to dwell on the past and build up layers of experience, and I suppose that's a whole Northern European way of being, as opposed to the American diffuseness or desire for novel experience.

DORN: I think you're right and it's precisely the thing I needed—and didn't dream could constitute that kind of articulation. And didn't realize that I didn't have to the extent that I did. A certain kind of approach to expression, I could almost put it, which was very linguistic and psychological, I got from Tom Raworth, another English person who I knew concurrently with Jeremy, although they inhabited different worlds. (They don't so much anymore—they both live in Cambridge, as it turns out.) Another aspect of my time in England that is more and more curious as I look back on it is Tom Clark's role as my teacher. I'm using the word "teacher" in the most latitudinous sense: what you learn from anyone. If you go through enthusiastically with someone something that turns you on (as we used to say) then that's a form of teaching. Tom had been doing graduate work with Jeremy and he came over with Donald Davie; we hung out together a great deal at Essex and, as an American who had been here for several years before I arrived, he taught me a lot about America in an area that… Because he was younger and was on to things that I hadn't actually read or had only heard of and hadn't really pursued. It was more in the line of poetry; for instance he was working on Pound and had gone into Pound in a much deeper way than I had. Hence it wasn't that the experience was totally English; the milieu of this country at that time was really open and brilliant. Looking back on it, that's how I feel it was. It may still be… But at that point in my life I gorged myself in a certain way on things that I hadn't had a chance to find before.

SELERIE: I'd like to pick up on this idea of hearing voices or a differentiation of tone. It seems to me that that accounts for a more dramatic quality in your writing at that time—the sudden intrusion of voices such as Fanon in poems about England.

DORN: Well Fanon was very prominent then. I was getting most of that from LeRoi Jones who quite frankly was another of my teachers. To be a poet at all I think one has to be blessed with a very fortunate convergence of voices at the time. You can struggle alone and you can do quite well but if you're fed these fabulous meals all the time it helps to create a distinctive and referable art—an individual voice which is nevertheless rooted in the mode of a social group or point in time. LeRoi Jones is another case of someone who had read deeply in areas that I had never had the advantage of studying—German, for instance. He had read Heidegger. Since he was keeping up on all the latest radical thought of his time, he passed a lot of that on to me. He gave me my interest in Dante and certainly the whole Fanon thing comes from him. He was a walking bibliography on what you should read in that area at that time—this is early sixties, mid sixties—so I brought a certain amount of that with me. I mean before I came over, from 1960 to 1965, we were heavy correspondents. Not so much after that, although we never really broke off relations with each other like the stories were supposed to indicate [laughter].

SELERIE: You've talked about the positive aspects of being in England but in that volume *The North Atlantic Turbine* there's a very strong critique of the staid quality of English life—the fact that people don't speak for themselves—and that is typified perhaps in the attitude of the Oxford students who say that "every substantive fit" is complete. They can't think of anything further to write and you suggest that if they can't find anything they should make it up, or that they should find by making up. You said in another interview somewhere that you feel that your view of England then was an "alien's take" and that you feel rather unhappy with the conclusions which you set out or imply in those poems.

But it seems to me, as a native Englishman, that in fact we needed that outside eye to provide a fresh and accurate picture of the society which had reached a point of crisis—I mean of possibility. *The North Atlantic Turbine* is much more reflective than a tourist postcard vision. It needed to be said in arresting language that this infinitely rich culture was also that which spawned the subjugation of the Red Man and notions of Manifest Destiny. You made that last comment—i.e. from the interview—in 1972 and it seems to me now, almost ten years later, you might want to qualify that viewpoint again in the Reagan-Thatcher era. You might feel that in fact the directness of statement there was very necessary and was valid.

DORN: If any young English person aspiring to make their way got something out of that then I'm happy for it. As I recall, the dissatisfaction voiced in the conversation with Barry Alpert was directed more toward my own sense of the form that my work might more happily for me take in retrospect. I thought it was a little thin, a little easy; it wasn't as helpful as it ought to have been and it took the form more of mere criticism, which in my view anybody with a certain amount of nerve might have been able to make—whether they made it or not.

SELERIE: But, as you said, that was the tenor of the age and you were in there as the antenna of the race—to borrow Pound's metaphor.

DORN: I suppose my dissatisfaction with that work was, and to a certain extent remains, that it's not up to what it should have been. It's rather metallic and quick perhaps. I don't think... Insofar as I think that still the Romantics are the worst thing that happened to English Literature—I mean not just for the English but for all English speakers—and I'm not really talking about how... You know, somebody might now say... I was reading H. G. Wells the other day and he was saying that with the exception of Shelley and so forth the whole thing is... in *The Shape of Things to Come*, which I can read in his context and say, "I don't have that much patience with Shelley." I think there's a certain thing that happened with the language which is now being paid for sadly and a certain egoism of expression which I find the main fault of this time. In that sense I feel that at that time I was recommending a certain kind of convention and parotting of conventions which would get poetry away from that kind of usage and which is what I felt that a lot of younger writers in England were doing at that time. I suppose that's what prompted that essay on Oxford. Also I came to feel later that there was a kind of chauvinistic Americanism lodged in it that I have since repudiated almost entirely, as through my education I came to see with a little more clarity the particular problems of both languages and how there are large areas in which the requirements or solutions don't overlap and how far in fact American has drifted off from the peculiar requirements of this island. In my maturity I realize that when a language goes through a difficult period it's just what a language does all the time.

SELERIE: Is that how you would now account for what you call "that inturned coldness / of the English man" ('Oxford: Part I: Fornication')? Do you feel now that that is more of a tourist take, an immediate reaction which is not based on familiarity with the culture?

DORN: Well not just a tourist take but... remember we are talking about the middle-late sixties in which it is now quite visible that Americans were filled with a kind of enthusiasm which gave them lots of quite impermanent ideas about the state of the universe and other countries and cultures, particularly the English one. Coldness? Again that was probably meant to define what I thought was a lack of nerve perhaps in the use of the language. But I think that that is nobody's business now except for the English.

SELERIE: I'm not sure that I agree with you there. Surely everybody has—

DORN: Well you don't have to [laughter]. In like measure I think the Canadians have their particular problems; they have to work them out. I don't think this thing we're calling English, which goes from Australia through Canada and the States to England significantly as the big bodies of speakers, really has that much to constitute a common... These types of English are compartmentalizations of a language; they are offshoots of a... they're getting more and more remote as they stretch their orbits and they drift off more and more, they get their own peculiarities. So how actually can one...? It isn't as if we're saying that there is such a thing as English Language and you will have any kind of dicta that will cover the whole range of it—that seems to me quite clearly not the point. Actually, if those four or five major departments of that language got to be more and more peculiar to themselves I think it would be beneficial.

SELERIE: That's interesting. Could you expand on that?

DORN: Yes I could. It seems to me the difference is between, say, such a language as French being the lingua franca, with this extremely stultified insistence that it be kept in bounds—there's always this Maginot Line against the intrusions, which aren't actually kept out by that means—and English which is a language which throve on intrusions from the beginning. English shouldn't have that closed attitude and in fact it doesn't. Now that English has replaced French as the lingua franca, the logical conclusion should be drawn: there is a kind of Esperanto people speak all over the world. This even drifts down into the major speakers; the way Americans speak in one sense is like Australian or Canadian talk. The English again are different because the source comes from a different kind of spring. But in the meantime I don't think that poetry has much to do with that development; I think it should cultivate its own peculiarities and not worry about its comprehensibility in that sense at all. In other words, what it needs to be influenced by is the passions which are strongest in the given area one might be speaking of, because it's all intercommunicable anyway. All these grosser categorizations that I'm making are certainly communicable—if you stop to think that really difficult dialects within English are even communicable.

SELERIE: This strength of particularity in language, which you feel should be more sought after, is presumably something that you are looking for in your reading of eighteenth century writers. Although one tends to think of the Augustan era as a time when a uniform poetic diction prevailed, I suppose it could be argued that Burns, Crabbe and Smart are at least as idiosyncratic as the Romantic poets. One can point also to the strength of the local in a poem such as *The Village*. Is it the particularity of language that is leading you to use eighteenth century writing as a model?

DORN: Well I hope I'm not modelling myself on the eighteenth century; to do that would become monstrous! But on the other hand there is an intensification and depth of rhetorical exploration in the writing of that period; there's a certain kind of motivation of the vocabulary that I think is so valuable to the ear. How much of that one can actually absorb and use is an important question because I think it would be dangerous to overdo it, to even allow it to become dominant in any way. Yet I find it an extreme sharpening apparatus, mainly for thinking, because they were thinkers and I haven't seen thinking like that; they were intentionally complicated and deep in that sense. I just find that so useful— it's like sharpening one's teeth if you're on the hunt for vocabulary, hunting for vocabulary. I just think—but on the other hand I let a certain amount of it drift in to my expression because I find it useful and I find that it has a certain intimidatory effect which I like, especially in a time of incredible euphemism and laxity of expression. So that's the way I use it. Other people, if they became interested, might use it in another way. I could see it being used with an ultimate grace and lightness. In a way you can see certain effects, not very admitted or publicized, in certain prose of the time. I think the best prose now refers more to the eighteenth century than it does to the nineteenth century. But that's really the nature of my interest in eighteenth-century literature; I don't go to that period for information, except information as to the manner and custom of language.

SELERIE: But at that period you went to the eighteenth century to find out about the origins of the United States, did you?

DORN: Oh I did, yes.

SELERIE: And you must have got interested in the sympathy of Wilkes and his supporters for the "Liberty Boys" across the ocean…

DORN: Because the United States is an eighteenth-century nation, as a nation, it's quite important to be aware of that process of events through the writings of the time, for sure. There's a certain kind of early American writing—I'm not talking about colonial writing but early national writing—that obviously shows all the effects of that and much of it shows some of the same kinds of abilities. Historically, that's quite true; it's a parallelism of great effect. For instance, Gibbon is one of the greatest aesthetic pleasures of my life—not only his style but his thinking I find nearly perfect.

SELERIE: Is it a kind of objectivity and balance which appeals to you—an ability to be simultaneously engaged and standing apart?

DORN: Objectivity is…

SELERIE: It's a dangerous word!

DORN: There are many kinds of objectivity. It can be totally dumb in a way but if it's objectivity—whatever that is—of loftiness and cast of mind, then I don't think I know of any language better for it than the last half of the eighteenth century.

SELERIE: It's almost like a simultaneous engagement with materials and an ability to stand above them and see their pattern as it's communicated to others.

DORN: Indeed, and I think it's the only really great load—even using that in the mining sense of like "the mother lode"—ever delivered to the literate public. I don't think, say, mid to late nineteenth century, because let's face it a lot of the first half of the nineteenth century was eighteenth century, except for the Romantics who were having their quarrel. What I find delivered there that is of most value and most worth remembering is a certain kind of emotional pitch and persuasion. Beauty? None really.

SELERIE: I noticed that you have Boswell's *Life of Johnson* over there. You've been reading that during your stay in London presumably.

DORN: Oh I read it all the time. Actually, I just picked up Boswell's *Hebrides Journal*.

SELERIE: It's interesting to compare that with Johnson's own account, isn't it?

DORN: It is, yes. Boswell is a much easier writer; he's more of a natural really because he's not particularly intellectual. Johnson is so complicated...

SELERIE: More concerned with the effect that he's going to make on the reader. Boswell has a more journalistic quickness of assumption.

DORN: And he's a simple spirit too.

FROM
JUNEAU IN JUNE
(1980–81)

Edward Dorn

Editors' note: The fragmentary text for this 'kind of journal' is contained in a folder called 'Alaska' in the possession of Jennifer Dunbar Dorn. It contains typed notes in various states of completion. The opening section, 'The Anthropology of the Denver/Seattle Flight', "got typed up on the computer" (J.D.D., email to Gavin Selerie, 5 November 2010). This has been used as the base text, with some transcription errors corrected by reference to Dorn's reading at the Institute of United States Studies, 16 June 1981. The typescript of 'Alaska Loca', probably envisaged as the second section, has a lot of handwritten corrections and additions by the author. These have been incorporated, after cross-reference with the London recording. Square brackets are present in Dorn's typescripts.

THE ANTHROPOLOGY OF THE DENVER/SEATTLE FLIGHT

Over sold tickets, aggressive duplication, fixed or dwindling seat numbers are the gems strung around the neck of the airline business, and what a neck they've got! Driving cattle to Market is an expression far too orderly and humane to apply to it. For those traveling [sic] "on the float," which is money the traveler's check people obligingly keep for you interest free (no usury there) or in broader, plastic cases, money not actually in hand but cast in some dark future (plenty of usury there), the take off roll is the moment when the customers receive their just deserts in the form of that abstractest of all services known as transportation.

Broiling on the ground in the casing of a 727 at Stapleton International were some hot sausages wishing they could lift off the grill. Even the stewardesses, those bastions of the dry forehead, were winking the salt out of their eyes. A boy in Juneau later told me we shouldn't call them Stewardesses, the new thing he said was to call them Stewardii, as in Waitrii and so on. But that's a couple of weeks in the future.

There are certain inane references in this kind of travel which would be far too routine to ignore. When the wealthy arrive in their private planes, that is said to be Jetting In, as in They Jetted in for the weekend. When the pedestrian fly they Wing In, or in the case of some obscure feeder lines I suppose, they still Prop In. Perhaps a linguistic relative of Pop In. And rarely for the weekend. Some of them will have brought the kitchen sink.

The first thing I do when I fly, after settling into my cheap sarcophagus, is straightaway pull out the company magaz. There is no single matter so helpful to Temporary Death, the sole companion of the air traveller. Within those glad pages the eyes become glazed cherries. Everything one needs from quartz to shwartz. This one is particularly heavy on the Pacific Rim, as it's called in higher circles. What constitutes High Pacific Rim and Low Pacific Rim (after the discrimination of high and low church) I was trying to discover when I began to realize that my right to a sarcophagus of any dimension was in question.

I had been late on arrival and had failed to notice that I got a go-ahead but no seat number. The agent had even smiled and said I didn't have much time. When I reached the gate I turned right on to the ramp and presented myself at the door of the plane. Since final preparations were in progress the personnel were making gestures which I interpreted as Pass On. I've travelled with as much frequency as any practiced amateur and should have received this glaring mistake but already I was preoccupied with the possibility of seeing the pumice of Mt. St. Helen's recent evacuation, the probably undisturbed ice-cream cone of Mt. Rainier and the general excitement of another Alaska adventure.

The back of the plane was full of restless smokers waiting for the take-off roll. I sat down in the last row of the nonsmokers just to be close to the smell at least of sotweed. Out the window the sweltering heat made liquid glass of the ground crew in their red white and blue jump suits as they swarmed over their hoses. On the other side the old 727 shuddered as it received the racks of predigested food into its belly. A lady with a hat on sat down in the aisle seat. Her face wore a costume of permanent irritation. She nervously checked her seat number with her boarding pass and I could see she had my seat, or perhaps it was reverse from her point of view. She was casting glances and gestures back up the aisle to what appeared to be the rest of her party. So it was not open seating. I rousted myself out, not to her relief, on the contrary, to her increased irritation.

As I stood in the aisle waiting for the trouble-shooter assigned to seats I became gradually aware of what in balmier days was called an altercation. A gaunt women with stringy hair clutched the broach on her dress while a Flight Attendant, hands lifted in the heat and eyes raised to the stars on the roof of the cabin, said

There are many aspirants but few seats and that the supervisor would be along any moment to untie this rat's tail. The other passengers turned, with insufferably secure demeanors, back to their individual, sleep promoting, matter.

But I was standing in the aisle, cranked entirely down from my brief hit of Company Magaz, Skiing in winter, living like a coconut on the beach, or screwing around like a buddhist the rest of the time. And Then I espied way at the other end, near what they still for some reason call the Cockpit, a frantic woman on the phone. She must, I thought have to be saying something like Hurry on Down Here! There's a knot on the Rat's Tail!

And then appearing very small at first, in trolleyed the Supervisor, a useless Gallicism for what was always The Day Man. I made sure to speak to him first, very quickly, very to the point and added I'd wait in front. He smiled with relief, and thanks, and then turned to address his bigger problem.

That stringy blonde woman had got on in Memphis. She was mad, she was right. The people who were about to usurp her sarcophagus were dressed in baby blue. Their mouths were set. They had been given every assurance they would ride. The blonde woman showed in her determination a flaw she herself was well aware of and was trying to plead her case on the basis of greater need. Witnessing such justification and knowing it would melt, I turned my head and made my way through the thriving business to the front door. As I moved the Day Man was leading the desperate creature into the aisle saying that, if she would just step out to the Computer he'd take care of her. A later flight no doubt. No! she shouted as he pushed her into the traffic, I don't want to go to the computer, I know I'll never come back.

One of the problems with air travel, from the traveler's point of view, is that there is no vocabulary of sufficient weight to maintain one's place. Up front they must say something if only switch on and switch off. The passengers can only make this stuttering attempt not to get thrown off once past the electric barriers. The onboard atmosphere of average airline is abject, to put the very least linguistic leverage on it. Everyone, even those who wouldn't ordinarily tolerate such intimidation assumes a mask of neurotic levity to hide their misery and dread.

But I knew all I needed to get a seat was to appear single. Who was to know that my family was to follow in three days time, that in fact I was an imposter. Add to that Extreme Patience, the most Inconspicuous Disbelief, a Full Shot of Smugness, and they would lead the way. I got a seat by the window. The second thing I do when I fly. Now there was no need at all to pay any attention to the Company Magaz. I opened my folder on Alaska and settled back into my sarcophagus as the pressure of the Take-off rolled me into focus.

ALASKA LOCA

> "It's like alcohol, tobacco and matches. None of it is necessary but it all works. At least it works in a fruit-fly, Judeo-Christian environment like ours. That another set of vices would work a lot better Cannot be gainsaid. Almost any other combination would do. But the powers of license have a particular interest in Those vices. And it isn't because They're neat and already in place. It is because they are Low Grade. In other words, the story of dope is not any different than the story of anything else. A lot of the Twiceborn think they're going to replace that triumverate with hard core prayer. Have you heard the Moral Majority broadcasts up here? What most people inside don't understand is that Alaska can produce anything. Our summer is lit by the most powerful Grow Bulb in the system. Matanuska Thunderfuck is only the crudest beginning."[1]
>
> — Anonymous Prisoner

To feel Alaska it is convenient to face the South. This should put your right shoulder on your West side. If you don't have a right shoulder, you can make one out of clay. Alaska is a shoulder in the way it is attached to the continent, with the Gulf of Alaska an armpit full of resources.[2] The salty smell of plenty, a bounty of crustacea and pisces which might seem tropical, but in regard to sea life tropical waters are relatively barren. Your right arm is at eight and you're facing South. You can see that you have a natural, if distant, relationship to Hawaii. Baranoff, the greatest of Russian rulers in the New World, ordered all his lettuces and turnips from there. He was a special friend of King Mau-Mau. But there were other lettuce farms in Hawaii, and they were all owned by King Luka-Luka. Before the Hawaiians were put in sarongs and motorboats they were very tough, they paid *very* close attention to how the Mountain shook, and of course with toughness one gets competition Direct. Baranoff wasn't always assured of his

---

[1] *Editors' note:* In his reading of this text at Buffalo, 24 March, 1981, Dorn provides a gloss on Matanuska Thunderfuck: "That's a kind of marijuana they grow up north of Anchorage. There's a place called the Matanuska Valley."

[2] *Editors' note:* A handwritten subscript "o" appears to be appended to the front-end of the word "resources" in Dorn's typescript.

lettuce supply. That he got involved in their petty wars will come as no surprise: The Russians even then were prone as we, their correlative, to get drawn down by local factions, and squat, local Deities.

Falling away from the underarm then is the ribby side, The Alexander Archipelago, named for Alexander I. Alexander started out as a liberal, and eventually became lunatic. He was "reared in the free-thinking atmosphere of the court of Catherine II." Rousseau, the traditions of Russian Autocracy, and from his father a theoretical love of mankind combined with a practical contempt for men. In 1801 he mounted the throne over the body of his murdered father. He was liable at any moment to issue an extravagant action. He sounds like most modern men would be if they had power. He was the admirer of Napoleon whom Napoleon invaded. He was quite defective. Altho he lamented the state of his inheritance and said his reign was but "a happy accident" and spoke bitterly of "the state of barbarism in which the country had been left by the traffic in men" and that "under Paul three thousand peasants had been given away like a big bag of diamonds," his love of liberty, if perhaps sincere in momentary passion, was unreal, and rarely, it is said, got appropriate application.

The Alexander Archipelago, or the Panhandle, is also called The Southeast. It is a northern extension of what in "the Lower Forty-Eight" is called The Northwest. It is all governed by a maritime climate stretching from Santa Barbara to the glaciers, but in the north the winter makes it more like Norway. Up here latitude is everything. It is a masterpiece of dreamy islands ranging in size from mere rocks, on which a tree or two dwells, to great slabs of forest infested with grizzlies preoccupied with their territory and who Never smile. Their ancient competitors, Haidas, Tlinkits, don't smile much either and for loosely the same reasons, but that's a consideration for later chapters.

To our West, across the Gulf of Alaska, is the Alaska Peninsula, the bicep of the arm which becomes the Aleutians, and which ends only when it reaches the waters between Japan and Siberian Russia in an enormously spaced series of bony fragments, a finger accusing and tracking the greatest land mass on earth. Out there is where the Russians pursued the Sea Otter practically to the last pair. In terms of mass usage, they were the goose down of their time, and obviously, hide is no less dangerous to lose than your feathers. At the tip of that finger is a nail named Atu, a rock of no great size surrounded by distempered seas. Beyond that is another world, a strange world of violence embedded in passivity named Japan. In our own society we sequester individuals who manifest such character. The Ice Line hangs in a sagging, irregular curve above Atu island.

On that island there is a tracking machine of such size a Dodge pickup truck would be a dust mote to its orb. But its capabilities are way beyond those of a pinball machine, even though the classification, amusement, is the same. It can track 50 objects the size of Ronald Reagan's head 3000 miles away, and keep separate track of all of them, at the same time. In other words, it must be nearly useless. The Russian basket ball teams can't take a shot without our knowing it. Its ingenuity is not worth doubting. It is Teledyne's best entry in The History of Mechanism Stakes. It is right up there with the pyramids, or at least the Ziggurats. This is an expensive "and not inelegant" fingernail. Of course it would be better if all such deliquescence were as open as a university planetarium. A lot of citizens might be encouraged to spend some time there instead of shooting Elk. Alas for the military that they have no sense of human betterment, because the military has some exciting machinery and it wld do the public a better turn to get them involved with it than all those fraudulent ads about how much you can learn if you join the army.

Let us leave the Far West of this ðing. Our armpit boils with fish and their concomitant pursuers. We now have the 200 mile limit to lighten the load of the greatest marine poachers on earth, the Japonese. Remember who invented the 200 miles limit. And remember why they had to lay such a broad claim on the seas, the first time in history since the Pope ran a line through Brazil. You are perfectly correct, it was the Peruvians, and it was to protect their Anchovies. Those anchovies were largely en route to the gullets of Battery hens laying somewhere in Alabama. And the Norwegians fell right in with their Smelts. Our act came somewhat later and probably due to pressure by those with a protein problem on the grand waters off New England. As things now stand the Russians may have been put off, but that the orientals have come in through the back door so to speak is attested to in the great bumper sticker DONT LET THE MOON RISE OVER GLOUCESTER. But most of that's been covered by Television.

What we can do here is take a Top Shot. Let's put our position a hundred and fifty miles over the Gulf of Alaska. We can assume another point of the same altitude over the center of continental Alaska. From the Gulf we can see the Prinsendam burning and ladies with blued hair from Pasadena being elbowed out of the lifeboats by nervous Filipino waiters, without the hint of an apology. It is a scene only the imagination of a Wm. Burroughs could capture. The gulls wheeling around the emergency is a scene only the imag of John Burroughs cld capture &c and the jungle-like urgency to save one's carcass only depictable &c by Edgar Rice Burroughs.

Around this piece of expensive damage helicopters buzz and lifeboats drift away, north toward Valdez (rhymes with sneeze) the shipping point at the end of the pipeline. And they drift toward Sitka on the east. Tugs arrive. It takes a while to put a line on her in the heavy seas. There are reckoned to be 200,000 gallons of fuel on board. At last she's in tow, lugging toward the Archipelago. And she starts to torque. For three minutes, one of the slowest turns for a thing that size the world has ever seen. When the bottom finally comes up, at the end of this monumental roll, she sinks into 9,000 feet of water.

THREE POEMS AND A DRAFT (1981)

Edward Dorn

Editors' note: 'How Small Can Awesome Get?', 'Further Thoughts on Dogs', and 'Let Those People Go', published in *Spectacular Diseases*, 6, ed. Robert Vas Dias (Cambridge, 1981), 30-2.

HOW SMALL CAN AWESOME GET?

When Caspar Weinberger
crossed the threshold
at Bonn airport
he tightened the knot
in his tie.

At a U.S. airbase
seventy miles north of London
he adjusted his tie
as he lowered himself
into the cockpit of an F-80,
duplicating the german gesture.

The signal is clear: nervous,
automatic, a compulsion
for utter finitude. And,
it could be
a preference for hanging.

Personage

When Caspar Weinberger
crossed the threshold
of ~~france,~~ germany he tightened the knot
in his tie. When he ~~entered~~
lowered himself in to the cockpit
at an airbase 10 miles n—
north of London, the symbolic touching
of the knot in his tie
duplicated the german Gesture.
The quality is clear: nervous,
automatic, a compulsion
for utter finitude. and,
it could be,
a preference for hanging.

                                  Boulder Co april $\frac{19}{81}$

Editors' note: 'Personage' (19 April 1981) [1 p., MS], Box 42, Notebook *The Joy of Nothing/by no one* (1981–93), Edward Dorn Papers, Archives & Special Collections at the Thomas J. Dodd Research Center, University of Connecticut Libraries.

FURTHER THOUGHTS ON DOGS
London 9 July, 1981

Now that evolution is down for the count
we are permitted to speculate on
the dog's lineage by other classifications.

Although in no way but common lungs
do they resemble each other, and although
the load delivered is usually incommensurate,
street pigeons and dogs, empiricism tells us,
are set the same task, being to bury civilization
under a progressive crust of offal
three metres thick. This coarse chutzpah
we can applaud but not approve.

Amsterdam's quaint beauty is made slippery
by this dogeon effluxion, and dangerous
by the cambered crust at the canal's edge.
Dumped on and dumped in by this disgusting diet
the city's sanity will be secured by riot.

LET THOSE PEOPLE GO

Sometimes I think
the only threat to human number
would be to erase their names.

Bombs don't scare 'em
Diseases are too slow
The larger fauna are too random
Earthquakes are too local
"Holocaust" is too selective
Greed too dispersed and general
and right to Life a hollow phrase.

Let 'em go! rings in the halls
of the citadel, They'll find
their own way to the end.

BIBLIOGRAPHY OF EDWARD DORN INTERVIEWS

Donald Allen, ed., *Interviews*, Writing 38 (Bolinas, CA: Four Seasons Foundation, 1980). [Six interviews: 1961-79.]

Tom Clark, 'Ed Dorn's Views' (February 1980), *Views*, ed. Donald Allen, Writing 40 (San Francisco: Four Seaons Foundation, 1980), 9-24.

With Charles Olson, 'Reading at Berkeley—The Day After' (24 July 1965), *Muthologos: Lectures and Interviews*, Revised Second Edition, ed. Ralph Maud (Vancouver: Talonbooks, 2010), 193-203. [This is the latest transcription of a discussion filmed by Richard Moore as preliminary footage for his National Educational Television segment on Olson in Gloucester.]

Harvey Bialy, Unpublished interview (11 November 1972), The Poetry Collection, SUNY Buffalo.

John Wright, 'An Interview with Edward Dorn' (4 September 1990), *Chicago Review*, 49.3/4 & 50.1, Edward Dorn: American Heretic, ed. Eirik Steinhoff (Summer 2004), 167-215.

Effie Mihopoulos, 'Ed Dorn Interview' (1991), *The Cento Pages*, online: http://epc.buffalo.edu/authors/dorn/DORN_CENTO/dorn_mihopoulos.html. [Revised as 'From Imperial Chicago' in *Ed Dorn Live*. In his unpublished Masters thesis, Kyle Waugh notes "the considerable and arbitrary liberties that Joseph Richey's volume, *Ed Dorn Live*, takes in editing Mihopoulos' interview with Dorn, altering the wording of questions and deleting entire sections of Dorn's responses".]

Kevin Bezner, 'An Interview' (1991), *The American Poetry Review*, 22.5 (September-October 1992), 43-6. [Revised as 'A Correction of the Public Mind', in *Ed Dorn Live*, where it cuts out opening exchanges that address the composition of *Gunslinger* and *The Cycle* particularly.]

Kevin Kaszubowski, 'Dorn on Dogs: An Interview with Edward Dorn', *Dog Stories*, ed. Kevin Kaszubowski (University of Colorado, 1993), 5-15.

Joseph Richey, ed., *Ed Dorn Live: Lectures, Interviews, and Outtakes*, Poets on Poetry (Ann Arbor, MI: The University of Michigan Press, 2007). [Roughly eight interviews and six lectures: 1977-99.]

Edward Dorn, *Two Interviews*, eds. Gavin Selerie and Justin Katko (Bristol: Shearsman Books, 2012). [1971/1981.]

BIOGRAPHICAL NOTES

EDWARD DORN, a prominent Black Mountain poet, 1929–99, came to life in "Villa Grove, Illinois, a small town on a secret confluence of the Wabash. He was born in the spring of the year of the very terminal October 29th. There was no flood that year, all the money having been carried off by a few men of vision. In fact that year was the beginning of a long spell of dry weather all over the world." That biographical note is taken from the hardback edition of *The North Atlantic Turbine* (1967). Dorn's *Collected Poems* are published by Carcanet Press. The bulk of his literary archive, up to 1993, is held at the University of Connecticut, while the archive dating mostly from 1993 to his death is held at the University of Notre Dame.

JUSTIN KATKO is from Lexington, Kentucky, and has studied at Miami University, Brown University, and now the University of Cambridge. He is one of the co-editors of Edward Dorn's *Collected Poems* (Carcanet Press, 2012), and he runs the small press Critical Documents. His recent books of poetry include: *The Death of Pringle* (Veer Books, 2011; Flim Forum Press, 2012); *Rhyme Against the Internet* (Crater Press, 2011); *We Are Real: A History*, with Jow Lindsay (Critical Documents, 2012); and *Songs for One Occasion* (Critical Documents, 2012).

GAVIN SELERIE was born in London, where he still lives. He taught at Birkbeck, University of London for many years. His books include *Azimuth* (Binnacle Press, 1984), *Roxy* (West House Books, 1996) and *Le Fanu's Ghost* (Five Seasons Press, 2006)—all long sequences with linked units. A New & Selected Poems, *Music's Duel*, was published by Shearsman Books in 2009. He is currently engaged on a project which dovetails the lives of Joe Harriott and Thomas Hariot: *Hariot Double*. His work has appeared in anthologies such as *The New British Poetry* (1988), *Other: British & Irish Poetry since 1970* (1999) and *The Reality Street Book of Sonnets* (2008). Selerie has collaborated with other writers, notably Alan Halsey in *Days of '49* (West House Books, 1999). In addition to these imaginative writings he has published critical essays and edited the Riverside Interview series (Binnacle Press, 1980–84). An article on Charles Olson's British contacts and line of influence will appear in *Contemporary Olson* (Manchester University Press, 2014). A fuller account of such activity is available at: http://www.archiveofthenow.org/authors/?i=123.

www.ingramcontent.com/pod-product-compliance
Lightning Source LLC
Chambersburg PA
CBHW030908170426
43193CB00009BA/775